LAST OF THE BLUE WATER LINERS

LAST OF THE BLUE WATER LINERS
PASSENGER SHIPS SAILING THE SEVEN SEAS
WILLIAM H. MILLER

The
History
Press

*To dear Evalee
Beloved friend, excellent
teacher, always valiant
and inspiring*

First published 2018

The History Press
The Mill, Brimscombe Port
Stroud, Gloucestershire, GL5 2QG
www.thehistorypress.co.uk

© William H. Miller, 2018

The right of William H. Miller to be identified as the Author
of this work has been asserted in accordance with the
Copyright, Designs and Patents Act 1988.

British Library Cataloguing in Publication Data.
A catalogue record for this book is available from the British Library.

ISBN 978 0 7509 8433 1

Typesetting and origination by The History Press
Printed and bound in India by Thomson

Cover Illustrations
Front: French artist Albert Brenet's brilliant depiction of the mighty
France at New York. (Moran Towing & Transportation Co.)
Back: Busy times! New Zealand Shipping Company's *Rangitiki* loading
in London Docks. (Mick Lindsay Collection)
Frontispiece: Midnight sailing from Southampton for the brilliant
United States. (United States Lines)
Page 4: The *Dominion Monarch* sails from the Queens Wharf at
Wellington on 5 March 1949. (ALF Collection)

CONTENTS

FOREWORD

As a young man fresh out of college in 1961, I made a summer trip to Europe. I decided to go by ocean liner – crossing over on the *United States* and home on the *America*. It was magic – the seas, the fellow passengers, the food and service, and of course the ships themselves. There was something very special, I felt, about the sense of a 'moving city' – this huge mass of steel moving across the Atlantic Ocean.

I was quite fortunate in later years – I attended two of Bill's wonderful lectures. He brought the liners, crossings and especially my own voyages back to life. After each, I was full of praise, and most grateful to Bill – he is the evangelist of ships!

Thank you, Bill, for your knowledge, your enthusiasm, your lectures and for books like this one.

Edward Coe
New York City
August 2017

INTRODUCTION

My scope here is very definite: the late 1950s and through the 1960s. In almost thundering drama, the airlines with their swift jets had arrived – first on the transatlantic run in 1958–9 and then, a decade or so later, to almost all liner trades including those east of Suez. In little more than a decade, it was the end of an era – the last class-divided passenger ships that carried travellers from point to point were, quite simply, no longer viable, and certainly no longer economic and profitable. They were replaced by all-one class, hotel-like cruise ships – 'floating hotels' as they were dubbed – and which often visited a collection of ports, which were often in the sun. The traditional passenger ships, many of which carried cargo as well, were doomed to extinction.

These passenger ships carried a variety of passengers, and often in starkly different quarters – from top-deck suites to lower-deck dormitories with as many as fifty berths. In those final years in the 1950s and 1960s, the great liners carried Hollywood stars and even royalty on the Atlantic, businessmen to South America and Africa, migrants to Australia and New Zealand, and, in reverse, visitors returning to European homelands. And, of course, there were the tourists – those crossing the Atlantic, say, between New York and Southampton, those heading to South Africa to escape Northern winters and, farther afield, touring the Orient.

This book is divided by chapter and includes another nostalgic review of not only the famed Atlantic liners, but many other passenger ships as well, each divided by region. Until the 1960s, there were still hundreds of passenger ships that plied trades around the world, so I cannot include all of them, or even all the ship owners. Instead, this book is an overview. It is yet another nostalgia-filled grand parade of a bygone maritime age.

Along with my own collection of books, articles and photos, I have gathered anecdotes of ships and those who sailed in them. Some of these anecdotes hopefully add and even spice up the pages of this book. Happily, I have also had the added resource of having sailed aboard some of the ships themselves, from the *QE2*, *France* and *Oriana* to the *Canberra*, *Achille Lauro* and *President Cleveland* – as well as ships that are much changed, but that once sailed as the *Kenya Castle*, *Southern Cross* and even the little *Aurelia*.

Almost half a century later, this generation of passenger ships are all but swept away completely. By the 1970s, jet travel had become more and more popular – and much more affordable. Instead of six daysfrom New York to England, it became six hours; similarly, twenty-one days from Southampton to Sydney changed to twenty-one hours.

Myself, I still miss that era, those ships and the services they provided. And so, coupled with facts and dates, herein is another round of recollections and reflections by crew members, historians, harbourside onlookers and, of course, the passengers themselves.

Bill Miller
Secaucus, New Jersey
Summer 2018

ACKNOWLEDGEMENTS

I have been very fortunate: I have been lecturing aboard passenger ships for some forty years. There have been countless trips – several hundred, in fact! – a long list of ships and itineraries and ports of call, and a long collection of titles, from the North Atlantic's floating palaces to the Cunard *Queens* to the port of New York. What great fun! The reward has been equally as great: I have so often met fellow passengers who, usually after these talks or during a teatime encounter, share stories of ships of all types, some famous and some quite remote. Diligently, I have copied and documented these. There are, in my files, hundreds upon hundreds of them. They come from captains, dining-room waiters and cabin stewards, passengers, deckhands and booking agents in downtown corporate offices. So I have dedicated this book to them with the greatest thanks. Their words and their stories have brought many bygone ships and shipping lines back to life.

Otherwise, and more specifically, I must thank a large 'crew' of assistants and contributors. Special thanks to Amy Rigg and The History Press for taking on this title. Special mention for prized photographs must go to Tony La Forgia, Tim Noble, Rich Turnwald and to Mick Lindsay for generously sharing his vast photo collection and those photos of Kenneth Wrightman and Dave Vincent. Thanks go to Michael Kenyon, Alan Parkhurst and Marco Roccalia for their extensive recollections, anecdotes and insights, and to Michael Hadgis for his technical assistance.

My crew of additional assistants has been extensive: Mary Louise Albert, the late Frank Andrews, Joann Bauer, John Bone, the late Frank Braynard, Mary Briggs, Stephen Card, Tom Cassidy, Gordon Cooper, Elizabeth Crossley, Captain W. Deijnen, the late Alex Duncan, Richard der Kerbrech, Alan Dunbar, Maurizio Eliseo, Richard Faber, Marjorie Gateson, the late John Gillespie, Pippa Gordon-Jones, Nico Guns, Sonja Haraldson, David Hutchings, Norman Knebel, John Lloyd, Anton Logvinenko, Hugh Markham, Captain James McNamara, Larry Miller, Jack Newman, Nick Newman, Mary Quinn, Robert Pabst, John Philipps, George and Alice Shaw, Martin Shawcross, John Simanski, Graham Spurrier, John Turner, David Williams and Derek Wood.

Companies and organisations that have assisted and provided materials include: British India Line, Crystal Cruises, Cunard Line, French Line, Holland America Line, Italian Line, Matson Line, McAllister Towing Co., Moran Towing and Transportation Co., P&O-Orient Lines, Shaw Savill Line, South Street Seaport Museum, Steamship Historical Society of America, Union-Castle Line, United States Lines, World Ocean and Cruise Liner Society and World Ship Society.

Any and all oversights are deeply regretted.

TRANSATLANTIC CROSSINGS: BETWEEN THE OLD WORLD AND THE NEW

1

Ship lovers are a special group. With our joint enthusiasm, interest and passion, we seem to meet and connect everywhere – at home, on board ships and in locations around the world. On a warm June day in 2016, I had lunch in Southampton, England, with a friend who had come down from nearby Winchester, and then we visited an ocean liner exhibit in the 1930s-style city centre. It was a superb presentation, highlighted by a very varied array of items and made more pleasant and pleasing since the museum is selling books by someone known as 'Mr Ocean Liner'.

The local powers had outdone themselves, in fact. The exhibit, done in several large rooms, was called *Port Out, Southampton Home*. Storerooms and warehouses must have been unlocked and unloaded; most items were perhaps seeing the light of day for the first time in a long, long time. Sensibly, the liners were grouped by decades, starting in the nineteenth century, but concentrating on the twentieth, and then coming forward to the present age of Cunard, P&O and Royal Caribbean mega cruise ships. Favourite liners such as the original *Queen Mary* and *Queen Elizabeth*, *Caronia*, *QE2* and *Queen Mary 2* were given special expanded attention, but really, just about everything was interesting. There were the likes of a Smoking Room chair from the Royal Mail Lines' *Alcantara* (1926), an oversized chair from the *Majestic* (1922) and a statue of Christopher Columbus that stood aboard White Star's *Homeric* (1922). (The *Homeric* was to have been the *Columbus* of North German Lloyd, but was given to the British as post-World War I reparations.) Then there was lots of china, cigarette boxes and ashtrays, photos of arriving celebrities, as well as an extensive menu collection. Varied printed matter abounded, along with paintings and lots of those wonderfully evocative, oversized posters. Notably, there were several of those really great, highly detailed models: the *Normandie*, *Andes*, *Britannic*, *Lancastria*, *Reina Del Mar*, *Windsor Castle* and (possibly the most spectacular) a huge rendition of the post-war, refitted *Alcantara*. Then there was the big brass bell from P&O's *Arcadia*, a model of the Ocean Terminal (opened in 1950) and the 41-foot-long paying-off pennant from the retired *QE2*. Clearly, we were enthralled. Yes, it was just spectacular! It was all glorious ocean liner memory lane.

A year later, in 2017, the Peabody Museum in Salem, Massachusetts, also did a superb, extensive exhibition on liners which then 'sailed' itself across the Atlantic and went to London's Victoria and Albert Museum. At their headquarters in Providence, Rhode Island, the Steamship Historical Society of America held a highly successful ocean liner banquet, themed to the immortal *Titanic*, and then to be followed with a sequel banquet in 2018, linked to the illustrious French *Normandie*. In New York, Sotherby's aroused great notice when auctioning glass panels from the French flagship. Yes, great interest continues.

Following the Second World War, passenger ships enjoyed a huge resurgence. It was back to business – people needed transport. These were traditional, classic passenger ships, class divided and usually carrying at least some cargo as well and adhering to strict scheduling. They were the links. They were the blue water liners.

These ships often played important roles in lifetime stories and in family histories, and remain strong in memories. Recently, a lady told me of her father emigrating on the Red Star Line from Antwerp to New York aboard the *Kroonland*. As she spoke of his journey, tears flowed from eyes. She thought of his great effort, the journey itself and passing through Ellis Island in New York. She would never forget the name *Kroonland*, and had found and bought a postcard of that ship on eBay. It was a link to her late father.

During a recent crossing on the *Queen Mary 2*, the last of the transatlantic liners, I typically met many passengers after my talks about ocean liners. They tell me stories, ask questions, recall something from their lives and their earlier travels. A grey-haired lady from Baltimore commented:

> I was hoping you would have mentioned a passenger ship named *Washington* in your lectures. It has a place in my family history. My father, Jewish and from Poland, was in five different concentration camps during World War Two. He lived on meagre rations of bread and water, but then one day collapsed in a long march. He was thrown on a heap of dead prisoners, but then suddenly moved, showed signs of life and was rescued by the other prisoners. He endured – and was liberated by American soldiers in 1945. A year later, he was pronounced ready to come to the United States. He was sent on a liner-troopship, the *Washington*. He told me that when he reached New York harbour, he saw the Statue of Liberty and the Manhattan skyline, bent down and kissed the wooden deck, and cried. It was his ultimate freedom.

Another, a retired professor, had survived the war in Europe and then come to New York from Le Havre on the austerity ship *Marine Flasher*. 'The ship was very basic, almost crude, the voyage rough and unsettling, and the food adequate, but it was the voyage of my family's lifetime. The *Marine Flasher* carried us to post-war America – to freedom, to opportunity, to a new life.'

A rare occasion: The two most famous and successful pair of Atlantic liners, the *Queen Elizabeth* and *Queen Mary* (departing), together at Pier 90, New York, December 1948. (ALF Collection)

New York's great Luxury Liner Row in a scene from March 1962. From top to bottom: *Atlantic*, *United States*, *France* and *Queen Mary*. (Port Authority of New York & New Jersey)

Early morning: the beloved *Queen Mary* in New York's Upper Bay, inbound from Southampton and Cherbourg. (ALF Collection)

By the late 1940s, passenger lists to and from Europe and New York, as well as the likes of Montreal and Halifax, were growing. The Hollywood stars, important politicians, businessmen and, most all, tourists were back – and in increasing numbers. There was also a post-war wave of immigrations – Europeans wanting more opportunity, a better life and, in some cases, freedom in America and in Canada. The Atlantic passenger ship business had a very promising future.

Mighty, well-known and historic, the Liverpool-based Cunard Line was the biggest to return, with the extraordinary *Queen Mary* and *Queen Elizabeth*, the two largest and fastest ocean liners afloat; the pre-war *Mauretania* and *Britannic*; the brand new, luxurious *Caronia* (commissioned in late 1948 as 'Britain's largest and most luxurious post-war liner'); and four aging survivors from the 1920s: the *Scythia*, *Samaria*, *Franconia* and *Ascania*. Cunard also restored the veteran four-funnel *Aquitania* (dating from 1914), but primarily for migrant and low-fare service, and added two new combination passenger-cargo ships, the 250-berth *Media* and *Parthia*. Another British company, Canadian Pacific, returned with the sisters *Empress of Canada* and *Empress of France*, and – bigger and fancier still – the three-funnel *Empress of Scotland*. The French resumed, first with the *De Grasse* and then the illustrious *Ile de France*, but then inherited (as post-war reparations), the giant ex-German *Europa*, which would be gloriously restyled as the *Liberte*. The Dutch had the likes of the *Nieuw Amsterdam* and *Veendam*, the Scandinavians with a few survivors (such as the 1918-built *Stavangerfjord* and the *Gripsholm* of 1925). The Germans were out, stripped of all surviving tonnage. From the Mediterranean, liners were few – Italy's *Saturnia* and *Vulcania*, and Greek Line's *Nea Hellas*.

Running at 28 ½ knots, the Cunard *Queens* were the fastest way to cross: five days between New York, Cherbourg and Southampton. Elizabeth Crossley from Bath in England crossed roundtrip on the *Queen Mary* in 1961. She recalled those swift five-day passages:

> I especially remember there was a Daily Tote, run outside the ship's shops at lunchtime. It was 50 cents to enter. It was a mileage pool based on the ship's noon reading. But at night, there was a sweepstakes. That was the big money and sometimes very big money, maybe as much as $100!

Many people were fascinated by the great liners, by the places they went, sometimes just by the sight of them. Now long retired, Alan Dunbar recalled:

> I worked for UPS at their facility at West 43rd Street and Twelfth Ave in Manhattan. It was just across from Pier 86 and where the *SS United States* berthed. I used to cross under the old West Side Highway and make quick visits, usually before sailing, to the *United States* and the *Constitution*, *Leonardo da Vinci* and the *France*. Visiting these great ships was the next best thing to sailing aboard them!'

Passenger Ships Departing from New York, January 1953

Sat Jan 24			
Noordam	Hol-Amer	Rotterdam	Noon
Ocean Monarch	Furness	Bermuda	3.00 p.m.
Maasdam	Hol-Amer	WI cruise	4.00 p.m.
Rio Jachal	Arg State	B'Aires	5.00 p.m.
Santa Margarita	Grace	Valparaiso	11.59 p.m.
Sun Jan 25			
Stockholm	Swed-Amer	Gothenburg	10.00 a.m.
Italia	Home	Havana	6.00 p.m.
Tue Jan 27			
Stavangerfjord	Norw-Amer	Oslo	11.30 a.m.
Atlantic	Home	WI cruise	4.00 p.m.
Wed Jan 28			
Independence	Am Export	Genoa	Noon
Cristobal	Panama	Cristobal	4.00 p.m.
Quirigua	Unt'd Fruit	Kingston	4.00 p.m.
Thu Jan 29			
Ryndam	Hol-Amer	WI cruise	Noon
Fri Jan 30			
Liberte	French	Le Havre	11.30 a.m.
Emp. of Scotland	Can Pacific	WI cruise	11.30 a.m.
Santa Paula	Grace	Cartagena	11.30 a.m.
Santa Isabel	Grace	Valparaiso	Noon
Mauretania	Cunard	WI cruise	3.30 p.m.
Andrea Doria	Italian	WI cruise	4.00 p.m.
Exochorda	Am Export	Alexandria	4.00 p.m.
Afr Endeavor	Farrell	Cape Town	5.00 p.m.
Santa Sofia	Grace	Barranquilla	5.00 p.m.

Others often had vivid memories of passenger ships at such ports as Southampton, Le Havre, Rotterdam, Bremerhaven, Genoa, Naples and Liverpool. 'When I was ten [in 1949], I was taken by my grandfather to Liverpool,' recalled John Lloyd. 'The *Britannic* was arriving. It was night and the ship was aglow in lights. It was magic! Then and there, I was intoxicated. I started to dream of going to sea.' He later joined Cunard and served aboard the *Queen Mary*, *Queen Elizabeth* and *Mauretania*.

After some early work in hotels, John Turner joined Cunard in 1958. He was nineteen and began as a junior chef:

> I applied on Wednesday, was interviewed and hired on Thursday, and shipped out on the *Sylvania*, bound for Montreal, on Friday. Afterward, I moved ships quickly. Next, it was to the *Parthia*, a smaller ship. But she was such a poor 'sea boat' – she'd go down at the Bar at Liverpool and not come up again until the Statue of Liberty eight days later. Next, it was to the *Britannic*, for her Liverpool to New York crossings and her sixty-five-day winter Meddy [Mediterranean] cruise.
>
> Cunard was a great, great company – and it was a great honour just to work for them. Canadian Pacific, also based at Liverpool, was considered second class. The likes of the Blue Funnel Line was even lower – being dubbed the 'China boats' by crews around the Mersey.
>
> New York City was a sort of fantasyland to British crews back then. The ships would often remain in port for five or six days. There was very little work on board then and so we'd go ashore. Myself, I often went to the Market Diner and the London Book Shop and, of course, to Macy's. I'd buy 45rpm records. Dwayne Eddy and Pat Boone were my favourites. And I'd buy Fruit of the Loom underwear. I also bought dress shirts from Macy's – and one of them lasted fifty years. I liked those pin-tab colours. Quickly, I became one of the 'Cunard Yanks', looking immaculate in trendy American styles, velvet collars, shirt and tie and highly polished shoes. We even polished the soles of our shoes with black polish. We looked different. When we got back to England, we were like superstars. We could have any girl. We were like stars – we'd been to America, to New York!

Life on the liners, especially below deck, created a different world. John was making $120 a month as a galley chef by the mid-1960s:

> As a child, I lived in a tiny bungalow with one cold tap. We queued for everything, even firewood. The toilet was out back and shared. Going to sea on the liners seemed better, a different world. But there was also harsh reality. For me, the old *Mauretania* was the hardest ship to work. She was all up-and-down and had no easy or straight access. She was also a very hot ship. Sometimes she was all but glowing. On Cunard, we called the passengers 'bloods'. The staff and crew wanted to suck them dry for tips. There was also lots of waste.

Right: Great occasion: The record-breaking *United States* passes the outbound *America* off West 36th Street in Manhattan. (United States Lines)

Below left: Morning sailings – the *Ile de France* (right) and *Berlin* (left) have left their berths in this 1955 view. The *Franconia*, *Queen Elizabeth* and *Andrea Doria* are in the background and still docked. (Port Authority of New York & New Jersey)

Below right: The 34,000-ton *Caronia*, seen here at Valletta, Malta, was considered to be the most luxurious liner afloat in the 1950s. (ALF Collection)

Left: Ocean-going splendour: The First Class Main Lounge aboard the *Queen Mary*. (Cunard Line)

Below left: Gathering: The *Queen Mary* is wedged between the *Sylvania* (bottom) and the *Leonardo da Vinci*. (ALF Collection)

Below right: Legendary Cunard service. (Cunard Line)

Dishes by the thousand were tossed from portholes. Sometimes, the dishes were stacked and then the whole stack would be pushed over and out the porthole. And sometimes even silver items including those big trolleys were pushed out. After second seating, the boys down in the galley were hot, tired and often half drunk. They were tired of washing and polishing. Meats and other goods were regularly stolen and sent home to families. Passenger portions were sometimes cut back. There was also great waste of food before we returned to Liverpool. Twelve miles out, we dumped all unused foodstuffs – including whole sides of beefs, freshly baked cake and untouched long loaves of bread. These could not be used in port or on the next voyage. It was a great shame, I always felt, that these could not be given to orphanages and the needy. There were also great working systems between waiters and cooks and the galley crews. The waiters would pass, say, $10 to the cooks for the better meats and best cuts. Some waiters had hard jobs. Some had six tables with eight people at each, which meant forty-eight meals to be served at breakfast, lunch and dinner. Some of the chefs were very snobbish, very superior, very grand. I remember one was with Cunard for forty-four years. Another wore diamond cufflinks while cooking. Some of the captains were nice, some were mean and some like gods. One captain sent his 'tiger' [personal steward] down each day to collect his favourite, a custard tart. We even made our own after-dinner chocolates. But we were never, ever allowed to make Jam Tarts. They were considered 'common' by Cunard. Cunard was also doily mad – everything had to have a white paper doily underneath.

I met Marjorie Gateson from Philadelphia in 2016. She was then on her seventh Cunard voyage, but the first six were made over fifty years ago. Over lunch on board the westbound *Queen Mary 2*, she recalled:

My aunt and uncle crossed on Cunard every summer. They'd sail from New York in July aboard either the *Queen Elizabeth* or *Queen Mary* and then spend two weeks in London and then two weeks with family in Scotland. They always travelled first class. It was all purposefully planned – they would catch the August westbound crossing of the famous *Caronia*, the Green Goddess. The *Caronia* made only two or three crossings each year from Southampton and Le Havre to New York. Said to be the most luxurious ship in the Cunard fleet, my aunt and uncle loved the *Caronia*. It was primarily first class and run like a big, floating country club. They felt the very best of Cunard's staff were on the *Caronia*. From year to year, barmen remembered how they liked their Martinis. It was truly like the best hotel in London – the ship was run to perfection. But when my uncle died in the early 1960s, my aunt very generously took me as her companion. On three summer trips, we repeated the process: We crossed over on one of the *Queens*, stayed in London and then Scotland, and then returned on that August sailing of the *Caronia*. I was a young girl then, but I do remember the *Caronia* being very luxurious, very proper, very British. It was a world of quiet and order, immaculate white linens and polished silverware, and where all the other passengers seemed to know one another. Yes, the *Caronia* was really like a great club – but a great club that moved.

Business boomed – and then boomed even further. Just about every steamship line was ordering, or at least thinking about ordering, new tonnage – or at least adding second-hand ships. Even new companies such as the Arosa Line and Europe-Canada Line emerged.

The mood was, by 1950–51, to look forward, and this often included a look towards bigger and bigger passenger liners. There was backroom talk that Cunard was thinking of another super liner, perhaps a third Queen – it was quietly rumoured that a 95,000-tonner would have gas turbine propulsion. Another quiet rumour was that American business interests, still thinking of the Second World War and using liners as troopships, were said to be wanting to build a pair of 105,000-tonners with a design that made them easily convertible from peace time to war use.

There were also rumours across the Atlantic. The French, for example, were said to be contemplating a pair of 75,000-ton Atlantic liners, the Dutch wanted a running-mate for the *Nieuw Amsterdam* (an idea that did in fact materialise by 1959, in the form of the 38,500-ton *Rotterdam*), and none other than the Swedish American Line was looking over ideas for 'two giants' for Gothenburg–New York service.

There were whispers even from the mysterious Soviet Union. It was said that Leningrad shipyards were already working on plans for two 50,000-ton 'proletarian ships', which would 'sweep aside the pretensions of luxury and make ocean travel easier and cheaper than ever before.' These ships would be based, to some extent, on the Nazi government's 'Strength Through Joy' ships of the late 1930s, but it would seem that nothing more than ideas occurred.

Even Vladimir Yourkevitch, famous designer in the early 1930s of the opulent *Normandie*, was said to be caught up in this post-war super ship enthusiasm. He was reported to have presented the French government with plans for twin 100,000-ton liners that could carry 5,000 passengers per crossing. In his proposal, cabins would be smaller (with showers instead of bath tubs to save space) and large cafeterias would replace the traditionally lavish restaurants. Altogether, there would be a low, one-class fare. He projected $50 per person for a three-day crossing between New York and Le Havre or Southampton.

There were other plans and schemes, in the late 1950s. In July 1959, more than six months after the first jets flew the Atlantic and airlines overtook the steamship lines, New York-based businessman and hotel owner Hyman B. Cantor signed a preliminary order with a Hamburg shipyard to study the feasibility of building two 90,000-ton liners for North Atlantic service. These ships would break all existing records: they would be the largest liners yet, carry 6,000 passengers each and have service speed of 34 knots. Costing a combined $160 million to build, they would offer the lowest fares on the Atlantic – $75 per person each way, but without meals; passengers would pay for meals in shipboard cafeterias. They were to operate, according to provisional plans, between New York, Zeebrugge and Cuxhaven. The first, the *Peace*, was to enter service in August 1962; the second ship, the *Goodwill*, would join in August 1963. Expectedly, there were financing problems and the project never materialised.

Two months later, in September 1959, businessman Edgar Detwiler entered discussions with a Dutch shipyard to build no less than four even larger ships: 120,000 tons and 1,275ft in length. They would carry 8,000 passengers each and have 2,000 crew. They would be slightly less expensive than Mr Cantor's proposed ships, at $65 per person per crossing, and would include meals. Using the then innovative engines-aft design, they would cross at 35 knots. Dubbed the American–European Lines, flying the Dutch flag, they were to be named *United Nations*, *New Yorker*, *Lisbon* and *Hollander*. The first pair, due in 1963–64, would sail between New York, Cobh, Plymouth and Amsterdam; the second pair between New York, Lisbon and occasionally on to Naples and Genoa. But again, there were financing problems, among others, and nothing came to pass.

Comparatively, it would take some forty years, in the mid-1990s, for a passenger liner to exceed 100,000 tons and, by 2016, to over 225,000 tons and 6,700 passengers. But these were all cruise ships – there were no discount fares, all meals were included and there were the likes of cafeteria dining.

In reality, the might, power and innovation were displayed by post-war America on the North Atlantic. The pre-war, 1940-built *America* resumed sailing in 1946, but then was a

The maiden arrival of the 683ft-long *Constitution*, arriving off Lower Manhattan in June 1951. (Cronican-Arroyo Collection)

The *United States* at Pier 86, New York. (United States Lines)

The *Constitution* has been repainted in all white and has a gala return to New York in the spring of 1960. (American Export Lines)

A busy summer morning: The *Independence* at the bottom, alongside the *France*, *Olympia*, *Atlantic* and *Leonardo da Vinci*. (ALF Collection)

grand prelude to the brilliant *United States*, a 53,000-tonner that was the fastest and probably most advanced Atlantic liner of all. Commissioned in July 1952, the 990-footer swept the seas with a three-and-a-half-day crossing between New York and England, reaching as much as 36.8 knots. The 1,928-passenger ship was the flagship of the American merchant marine and her owners, the United States Lines. For the New York–Mediterranean run, American Export Lines added, in 1951, the 23,500-ton sisters *Independence* and *Constitution*. Sleek and modern, these sisters ranked as the first fully air-conditioned luxury liners. 'In 1959, I was a crewman on board the freighter *American Forwarder*,' recalled John Simanski. 'We plodded across the Atlantic from Le Havre to New York at 16 knots. But during that voyage, I had one of my proudest moments, both as a seaman and as an American. The *United States* swept past at 33 knots. I was very proud. That ship, her great design and amazing power symbolized America to me!'

The French returned from the ashes of the war and with a much-reduced fleet of passenger ships, beginning with the 17,000-ton *De Grasse*, then the splendidly restored *Ile de France* and *Liberte*, then the new, smart-looking *Flandre* (in 1952) and finally the brilliant *France* in 1962. That latter ship, at 1,035ft in length, ranked as the longest Atlantic liner ever.

Far left: Gala occasion: The maiden arrival of French Line's *Liberte*, August 1950. (ALF Collection)

Left: An evocative view: the *Liberte* caught in fog, captured off the French coast. (Author's Collection)

Afternoon sailing: the mighty *France* departs on her return maiden voyage from New York to Le Havre. (Moran Towing & Transportation Co.)

Mary Louise Albert began her sea travels in 1959, on board the great French Line and three of its ships, the *Liberte*, *Flandre* and then the *France*. 'They were all beautiful ships, splendidly decorated and a touch of France on the high seas. They each had great style, an ambience, but the greatest feature was the cooking. The food was beyond compare. They had to be the best-fed ships on the Atlantic. I always gained weight on a French Line crossing.'

The North German Lloyd resumed liner service in 1955, while the Scandinavians had the Norwegian America and Swedish American lines.

Sonja Haralson was born in Norway, but her family migrated to America in the 1950s. They settled first in Bay Ridge, Brooklyn, the big Norwegian community for New York City. After one of my talks on the great liners aboard the cruise ship *Crystal Symphony*, Sonja came forth and recalled:

Poland's *Batory*, built in 1936, takes a turn in a Halifax shipyard for her annual refit. (Author's Collection)

A maiden arrival: the brand new *Bergensfjord* arrives in the Lower Hudson River in this view from May 1956. (Cronican-Arroyo Collection)

My family and myself, then a small child, sailed to New York for the first time on the *Stavangerfjord*. It was an old, but very famous ship in Norway. I seem to recall it dated from World War I. We landed at Pier 42 in Lower Manhattan, in Greenwich Village I think. We returned to Norway a few years later on a sort of family reunion trip. We went over to Bergen on the *Oslofjord* and then returned on the *Bergensfjord*. They seemed like very big ships then, very luxurious and very exciting. I have kept postcards from those three Norwegian liners. They are part of family history.

Being in Italian waters, with visits to Genoa and Naples, has always prompted for me recollections of the great Italian Line, revived after the Second World War and continuing in the passenger ship business until 1977. Some memorable ships include the restored *Saturnia* and *Vulcania*, two flat-stack motor ships that, as I recall, had very period, very dark and very cramped passenger quarters for some 1,400 passengers each, and which traded on an extensive mid-Atlantic service: Trieste, Venice, Patras, Palermo, Messina, Naples, Barcelona, Gibraltar, Lisbon and Ponta Delgada over to Halifax and New York. Going eastward, they skipped Halifax and instead called at Boston for extra passengers. Then there were the handsome, all-white sisters *Conte Biancamano* and *Conte Grande*. They lost their hyper-Italian decor of the 1920s and were restyled extensively in the late 1940s as very contemporary, even modern ships. After the Second World War came a handsome series of brand new liners: the *Augustus* and *Giulio Cesare* of 1951–52, then the *Andrea Doria* and *Cristoforo Colombo* of 1952–54, and finally the superb *Leonardo da Vinci* of 1960. The Italian Line fleet was all but completed by 1965, with the first appearances of the *Michelangelo* and *Raffaello*. The big Atlantic liners were generally used on what was dubbed the 'express service' – Naples, Genoa, Cannes and Gibraltar to New York. The passenger lists were still very varied: from Kim Novak, Gloria Swanson and Loretta Young to the widowed Duchess of Windsor, the King of Morocco and, of course, small armies of hierarchy from the Catholic Church. The cardinals even brought their personal chefs among their entourages and all while the company thoughtfully flew their princely pennants from the ship's main mast. Lowly priests and nuns went below deck, in tourist class, along with the last waves of westbound Italian immigrants heading to North and South American shores. New lives and better opportunity beckoned for most of them. Until 1964, Italian liners were positioned at the bottom end of Manhattan's Luxury Liner Row, at Pier 84, at the foot of West 44th Street. Their ships often featured in the great 'stack ups' of liners at New York in those days but later moved to Pier 90, at 50th Street, which had just been vacated by Cunard. All of these Italian ships were very modern, class-divided liners, highlighted by their tiered, aft lido decks with pools, umbrellas and reclining chairs. The Italian Line also had a great style: Italian crews, Italian cooking and heaps of Italian charm.

Right: From above: the beautiful *Nieuw Amsterdam* arrives in New York in March 1957. (Flying Camera Inc.)

Below left: Holland America's *Statendam*, completed in 1957, was considered one of the best looking of all modern Atlantic liners. The 642ft-long ship is seen here docked with the British educational cruise ship *Dunera*. (ALF Collection)

Below right: Sweden's new *Kungsholm* (right) of 1953 passes the outbound, veteran *Gripsholm* of 1925. (Cronican-Arroyo Collection)

An afternoon meeting: the *Michelangelo* arrives at New York's Pier 90, with the *Leonardo da Vinci* on the left. (Moran Towing & Transportation Co.)

The *Raffaello* and *Michelangelo* at Pier 90, New York in a photo from January 1969. (Moran Towing & Transportation Co.)

Jack Newman crossed the Atlantic several times with his family back in the 1950s and '60s:

We would go to Europe in summer when my brother and I had school vacation. Usually, by the end of June, we were at sea. My father liked the Mediterranean, the warmth and sunshine and the foods of Spain and Italy. He worked in Manhattan but liked to go Downtown, to Lower Broadway and the shipping offices, collect schedules and rate lists and then plan for the next summer's trip. They were usually one-month trips – two weeks ashore in Europe and two weeks for traveling back [and] forth on ships. It all had to do with timing and my Dad's business schedule. We'd sail on all sorts of liners. There were different combinations each year. One year, we went over on the *Independence* and came home on the *Saturnia*. Another year, it was the *Constitution* over and return on the *Cristoforo Colombo*. One year, we went farther east, to Greece and the Holy Land, and then we sailed over on the *Queen Anna Maria* and returned on board the *Shalom*. Other ships we crossed aboard were the *Michelangelo*, *Atlantic* and a very old ship, the *Queen Frederica*.

Another pre-war liner, the twin-funnel *Conte Biancamano*, was pressed into busy, post-war service. Mary Briggs from Virginia recalled:

In 1956, we went to Europe, sailing to Italy on the *Conte Biancamano*. It was a wonderful Italian ship – wonderful Italian food and a very happy ambience. I especially remember the masquerade party. But the stewards and waiters were charming and often very good looking. It was a young girl's romantic paradise. I thought I was in love at least two or three times. We visited Rome and attended a blessing with Pope Pius XII. We toured Italy, went to the French Riviera and then met the *Vulcania* [also Italian Line] at Barcelona and sailed home. It was all just wonderful – and wonderful memories.

My very first visit to Cannes was back in the summer of 1973. We called there on a crossing to New York (from Naples and Genoa, and later stopping at Barcelona, Gibraltar and Lisbon) on board the big Italian liner *Raffaello*. We tendered ashore as the ship itself was anchored, and in the silhouette of the late afternoon sun, offshore. A barge had come alongside the *Raffaello* and loaded a mountain of luggage into the liner, along with a dozen or so big American cars and, as I seem to recall, one or two Rolls-Royces. There was a fireworks display that evening. When the lights of the moored *Raffaello* were switched off, that long and slender ship was even more of a silhouette. We finally sailed off at midnight – and for me, the second part of a transatlantic roundtrip that began with a crossing from New York to Le Havre on the legendary *France*. It was a special summer. But, of course, it was the great twilight for those long-standing Atlantic liner services – and I was very grateful to make voyages on two of the final French and Italian liners. It was the last goodbye to class-divided quarters, bullion at eleven, writing rooms and that determined, often electric, sense of purpose given to those passenger liners. Like a great train trip, you had a sense of destination – you were going somewhere!

The 1950s also seemed to usher in a great demand for economy in shipboard travel, but economy with comfort. Consequently, and as cabin class quarters soon disappeared, tourist class accommodation expanded. When Holland America Line introduced their new, 15,000-ton, 875-passenger *Ryndam* and *Maasdam* in 1951–52, a noteworthy 90 per cent of their passenger quarters were in tourist class – and as cheaply as $20 a day in a four-berth room down on D Deck. It was hugely popular – there were tourists on tight budgets, families, and students in summer.

In 1958, Captain W. Deijnen was assigned to his first passenger ship, the 15,000-ton, 875-passenger *Ryndam*:

> We sailed the North Atlantic between Rotterdam, Le Havre, Southampton, Cobh and New York (and sometimes stopping at Halifax). I remember that we took on lots of Irish immigrants at Cobh. All of them boarded by big tenders in outer bay. Originally intended to be a combination passenger-cargo ship [the sixty-passenger *Dinteldyk*], the *Ryndam* was redesigned as a passenger liner while under construction. She had only one screw and which made her very, very slow. She was listed as doing 16 knots at top speed, but actually she made only 14-15 knots at best. She was also top heavy – and so she was not a very good 'sea boat'. She was really terrible at sea – and was known by the officers and crew for terrible pitching.

Alternately, some Atlantic travellers enjoyed the club-like setting of a passenger-cargo ship, carrying 100–200 passengers in a first-class setting. There was the likes of Cunard's 250-berth *Media* and *Parthia*, American Export's *Four Aces* and Holland America's *Noordam* and *Westerdam*. Captain Deijnen served on the 134-passenger *Westerdam*, a large combination passenger-cargo ship. 'She was like a yacht. Very cosy and very comfortable. She too was rather slow [16 knots] and took nine days to sail from Rotterdam direct to New York [Hoboken before 1963].'

Other lines on the North Atlantic run included Canadian Pacific, Donaldson, Europe–Canada, Gdynia America, Home Lines, Arosa Line and, venturing into the Great Lakes, Holland's Oranje Line. The Mediterranean run included the likes of the Greek Line, Zim Lines, Spanish Line and – servicing Florida's then smallish Port Everglades – Portugal's Companhia Colonial.

There were troubled waters and times, of course. The liners sailed to very exacting schedules – often passengers depended on these – but occasionally there were delays and disruptions caused by bad weather, engine trouble, or even maritime, dock and tug strikes. Occasionally there were accidents and disasters. The *Empress of Canada* burned and then capsized at Liverpool in January 1953; the Greek *Neptunia* went aground in November 1957 and became a total loss; the *Maasdam* nearly sank after a collision with a sunken freighter in

Above left: Former Canadian Pacific liners at Miami, the *Mardi Gras* (ex-*Empress of Canada*) and *Carnivale* (ex-*Empress of Britain*). (Rich Turnwald Collection)

Above right: decor: the Smoking Room on the 1956-built *Empress of Britain*. (Rich Turnwald Collection)

Left: The beautiful *Nieuw Amsterdam* undergoing repairs at Schiedam, Holland, alongside the passenger ships *Indrapoera* (below) and *Fairsea* (top). The incomplete *Diemerdyk* is at the very bottom. (ALF Collection)

Right: A mid-Atlantic rendezvous: The *Saturnia* (at sea and bound for New York) passes the Mediterranean-bound *Vulcania*. (Italian Line)

Below left: Italian sensations: The *Cristoforo Colombo* and *Andrea Doria* at their homeport of Genoa. (Author's Collection)

Below right: The heavily damaged bow of Sweden's *Stockholm* following her fatal collision with Italy's *Andrea Doria*, on 25 July 1956. (ALF Collision)

A first-class double on the *Statendam*. A seven-night crossing from New York to Rotterdam was priced at $450 in high summer season. (Holland America Line)

Germany's River Weser in February 1963; and the *Hanseatic* caught fire at her New York pier in September 1966. However, the biggest blow was the loss of Italy's *Andrea Doria* in 1956.

The tragic collision and then sinking of the *Andrea Doria* on 25 July 1956 remains one of the most famous maritime disasters of the twentieth century. Myself, I well remember the television newscasts and newspaper headlines on the morning of the 26th: the *Doria* had been rammed the night before by another liner, Sweden's *Stockholm*. It all seemed too sad, tragic, almost incomprehensible. Even I was in disbelief. How could the *Andrea Doria* sink? Perhaps it was all a mistake. Still a schoolboy, but already a devoted follower and observer of the great liners, I was puzzled. I asked a special favour of my father: would he take me by car a day later (the 27th) from Hoboken to the cliffs of nearby Weehawken to make absolutely sure that the *Andrea Doria* had not arrived? She was due at Pier 84, at the foot of West 44th Street in Midtown Manhattan and just across from Weehawken, on the morning of the 26th. Soon after we arrived, I looked across. Even in the fading light of a summer's evening, the berth at Pier 84 was indeed empty. The *Andrea Doria* had not arrived as scheduled. Yes, she had sunk – the news reports were correct. Some thirteen New York City blocks north, the smallish,

Above left: The West German-flag *Hanseatic* prepares to sail from Cuxhaven for New York via Southampton and Cherbourg. (Hamburg-Atlantic Line)

Above right: Israeli registry: Zim Lines' *Israel*, a combination passenger-cargo liner, berthed at Haifa. (ALF Collection)

Right: Proud occasion: the new flagship of the Greek Line, the smart-looking *Olympia*, arrives at New York for the first time in October 1953. (Cronican-Arroyo Collection)

all-white *Stockholm* was in port. She had returned after having made an 11:30 a.m. departure two days before, on Wednesday the 25th. She was again at Swedish American Line's terminal, Pier 97 at the foot of West 57th Street. She had not been due back in New York harbour for another month, in late August. The *Stockholm* was never one of the more imposing Atlantic liners – she was actually more of a passenger-cargo ship – but she seemed especially small on that July evening. Like a bad child, she almost seemed to be hiding, in disgrace, fearing punishment. To most, she was already the villain, the less important little ship that sank the very important flagship of the entire Italian merchant marine and one of the post-Second World War era's finest new ocean liners.

In July 2016, a large, enthusiastic and very interested crowd gathered at SUNY Maritime College at Fort Schuyler, New York (just northeast of Manhattan itself) to commemorate sixty years since the sinking of the legendary *Andrea Doria*. There were a hundred or so in all – divers, survivors, relatives of survivors, assorted maritime gurus, school staff and of course a good dose of ocean liner buffs. There were even two ladies who had been aboard an important rescue ship, the legendary *Ile de France*. And there were other speakers, exhibits of salvaged items (from brass fittings from the *Doria* to delicate teacups), other assorted memorabilia from the ship and the Italian Line, a luncheon, a tour of the school's superb model and artefacts collection and then, like good sailors from Genoa itself, some of us went back to sea (well, sort of), for a short ride in recovered Lifeboat #1 from the *Doria*. The 26ft-long boat has just been fully restored and was all but spanking new. Rather appropriately, I also launched my new book, entitled *Andrea Doria and Other Recent Liner Disasters*. Afterwards, the lifeboat itself would make its way to Detroit, travelling overland by truck, for the premiere of a brand new docudrama on the *Doria–Stockholm* collision all those sixty years ago.

The airlines carried as many passengers as Atlantic passenger ships by 1957. A race began, but then changed dramatically by the fall of 1958, when the first of the very fast jet aircraft began crossing between London and New York. Within six months, the airlines had two-thirds of all transatlantic travellers, and this only grew: within five years, by 1964, the airlines had a 98 per cent share. Shipping lines attempted to compete, but struggled. By the mid-1960s, changes occurred, mostly the reduction of services and the withdrawal of liners; Cunard alone had retired four of its passenger ships by 1965.

The jet was not, however, the only problem passenger ship owners faced – it was also faced with increasingly troublesome and expensive labour. Strikes became more frequent by the 1960s, and Britain certainly had its share. The Great British Maritime Strike occurred in May–June 1966. Some 95 per cent of the still vast British merchant fleet was idle for six weeks as 55,000 seamen went on strike. Whole fleets stopped. In Southampton alone, there were five Cunarders, six ships from Union Castle and five from P&O; unique but sad sights. The British shipping trades never quite recovered. Over the next ten years, long-standing companies like

Union Castle, Shaw Savill, Furness-Bermuda, New Zealand Shipping, Ellerman and Blue Star all pulled out of the passenger ship business. Within another ten years, whole companies had closed down and vanished as well.

John Turner remembered:

The big British Maritime Strike in May 1966 was the turning point. I was on the *Carinthia* at the time when suddenly the Union steward came aboard a half-hour before sailing, we were almost ready to go, and he said, 'Get off.' The strike lasted six weeks. It was devastating. I recall that Cunard hired scabs, brought over from Newcastle in furniture vans. But most of the ships were idle – and Cunard and other lines lost millions. Things were never the same again.

John's last Cunarder was the *Franconia*, then on the Southampton–Montreal run, in 1967. Afterward, he turned to shore-side work – to bakeries and supermarkets.

The Atlantic liners left an indelible impression. It continues to this day, but in cruising. In fact, more people are sailing on passenger ships than ever; over eighty cruise ships were being built or on order by mid-2017. Great and continued growth is predicted. It brings to mind this charming verse I saw while in a travel office in Southampton in 2016. It is about the end of one trip, but the desire/need to continue and do more:

During the British maritime strike of May–June 1966, the *Carinthia* and *Caronia* are nested together at Southampton while in costly lay-up. A rare image. (ALF Collection)

Wanderlust lives in a suitcase
Empty now, except for a few grains of sand
Tiny sea shells, perhaps
Or a forgotten sugar sachet
in your pocket
The heart takes off
and beats for a moment
Somewhere far away
Another holiday soon, please
Unpack!

SUNNY SHORES: THE CARIBBEAN AND SOUTH AMERICA

2

Royal Mail, Blue Star and Pacific Steam Navigation Co. dominated British service to and from South America. Derek Wood recalled:

I worked for PSNC [Pacific Steam Navigation Co.] in the 1950s, aboard their two luxury liners, the *Reina del Pacifico* and the *Reina del Mar*. They were beautiful ships, but had a long run all the way from Liverpool over to the Caribbean, then the Panama Canal and down to the bottom of Chile. A roundtrip took over two months. I remember a storm off Bermuda when the *Reina del Mar* was thrown about, her twin propellers lifted out of the water and when we all but ran out plates. There was lots of breakage. My job on board one voyage was to train waiters. I had worked for Cunard before and I had the most experience. In the late fifties, PSNC was finding it difficult to get waiters on that long South American run and so had to hire lots of inexperienced staff.

Other passenger companies that served the Caribbean and South America included the Grace Line and Moore-McCormack Lines (from New York); Delta Line (based in New Orleans); Fyffes Line, Grimaldi-Siosa Lines, French Line, Royal Netherlands Steamship Co. and the Spanish Line (all from northern Europe); and from the Mediterranean, the likes of the Italian Line, Ybarra Line and Costa Line. There was also the Argentine-flag Argentine State Line and FANU Lines.

Airline competition and the gradual decline of immigration brought about an end to South American liner services. Maritime author Richard der Kerbrech recalled their twilight of years:

I travelled on the *Cristoforo Colombo* during March 1976 from Trieste to Lisbon via Naples, Genoa, Cannes and Barcelona. She was then on the Italian Line's South American run. I think the ship was about a quarter full. The Italian crew and the stewards were by this time paid very good wages across the Italian merchant service. Hence they were no longer reliant on tips. To this end the service was indifferent, the menu not too varied (mainly pasta based). Some staff were, to my mind, a bit taciturn. The cabin was clean but some of the mosaics in the shower were showing signs of deterioration and were breaking up. In the late evening, cold meats from the day were placed on a table on the Promenade Deck in the form of an open buffet. It was this time that cohorts of cockroaches would march along the decks. This is NOT an exaggeration and the crunch of them under foot was quite upsetting. This was the nightly routine although the wooden deck was really clean. For the entire voyage, the *Cristoforo Colombo* had a 4-5 degree list to starboard (as I recall). I felt I had come upon the Italian Line on the wane, and I think I probably had. Quite a contrast to their service of the '50s and '60s. Sorry to submit a bad report but I had such high expectations.

Included in this chapter is also an alternate way to/from Europe and the North American West Coast, but which included the Caribbean and Panama, offered by the Holland America Line. In the 1950s, the company had five passenger-cargo ships – the *Dalerdyk*, *Dongedyk*, *Duivendyk*, *Diemerdyk* and *Dinteldyk* – in this service. The routing was port-filled and so quite extensive: Hamburg, Bremen, Rotterdam, Antwerp and London and then across to Bermuda, Curacao, Panama, Los Angeles, San Francisco, Portland, Seattle, Victoria and Vancouver.

Captain W.J. Deijnen was posted in the late fifties to the fifty-passenger *Dongedyk*. 'She was an older ship, dating from the late twenties, but refurbished and updated after World War II,' he remembered. 'The *Dongedyk* was used in our North Pacific Coast service. Each voyage took sixty days – nearly two months.'

Below left: The 1932-built *Santa Rosa* maintained Grace Line's New York–Caribbean passenger trade until replaced by a brand-new *Santa Rosa* in 1958. (ALF Collection)

Below right: Holland-America Line's combo ship *Dinteldyk*. (Author's Collection)

Cosy quarters: the bar-lounge on the fifty-two-berth combo ship *Dalerdyk*. (Holland America Line)

Italian fleet-mates: on the South Atlantic run, the westbound *Augustus* passes the eastbound *Conte Grande*. A rare image. (ALF Collection)

Italian moderne: the First Class
Main Lounge onboard the
1952-built *Augustus*. (Italian Line)

The handsome *Augustus* waiting
between voyages at Genoa.
(Cronican-Arroyo Collection)

A busy day at Genoa: the *Augustus* (left), *Amerigo Vespucci* (center) and *Andrea Doria* together in their home port. (ALF Collection)

Restored after the Second World War in 1948–49, the *Conte Grande* had been built in 1927. (Italian Line)

Post-war British decor in the Smoking Room-Lounge aboard the fifty-passenger *Argentina Star* of London-based Blue Star Line. (Gillespie-Faber Collection)

Very attractive post-war first-class decor, as seen in the Smoking Room on board the *Conte Grande*. (Italian Line)

Costa Line's first new build was the 20,416-ton, 606ft-long *Federico 'C'*, completed in 1958. She is seen here at Genoa, with the *Bianca 'C'* just behind. (Maurizio Eliseo Collection)

A dual departure: Moore-McCormack's *Brasil* at Pier 97 and her sister *Argentina*, who has already been undocked and is about to depart. (ALF Collection)

3 SOUTHERLY COURSE TO AFRICA

iner services between Europe and Africa had their final boom in the 1950s and 1960s. De-colonisation, a shift to container cargo shipping and, of course, airline competition were among the contributors. Britain's Union Castle Line was the biggest and perhaps best remembered, but there were also the likes of British India, Elder Dempster, Ellerman, Belgian Line, several French companies and Portugal's Companhia Colonial and Companhia Nacional.

Union Castle had no less than thirteen passenger liners in 1960 and all of them in African service. A junior purser, who served on the SA *Oranje* (the former *Pretoria Castle*) and the company flagship, the *Windsor Castle*, recalled the main routing:

Southampton via Las Palmas or Madeira to Cape Town, Port Elizabeth, East London and Durban. It was called the Cape Mail Express. We carried about 200 passengers in first class [with another 500 or so in less expensive, lower-deck tourist class], but sometimes we'd have 100, even less in first. But the trade was slowly fading by the late Sixties. British and South African Airways had arrived and turned it from 14 days by ship to 14 hours by air. Just about everyone was defecting or so it seemed. But we still had some of the top-drawer business people sailing as well as South African government officials. In winter, there were also wealthy tourists in first class, people going on long holidays for two and three months, and often staying the whole time at the Mount Nelson Hotel in Cape Town. The ships were well known to them. They'd sail year after year, winter after winter. They were escaping the dreary, dark English winters, of course. We also had some great and memorable characters. One lady slept, according to her stewardess, with all of her valuable jewellery still on. Another, a man, asked if we could build him a new wooden leg during the voyage. Old Princess Alice [Queen Victoria's last surviving granddaughter] used to spend the day in a deck chair aboard the *Windsor Castle* while 'smothered' in steamer rugs. A very tiny, very elderly lady, she'd almost disappear. And there was one elderly couple I recall. They'd stand in the ship's foyer, but both under open umbrellas. When gently probed, their answer was always the same and always quite firm: 'They were in the park, feeding the birds and, of course, it might rain!'

Post-war sensation: The 747ft-long *Pretoria Castle* and her sister-ship, *Edinburgh Castle*, were Union-Castle Line's biggest, fastest and finest post-war liners. (Union-Castle Line)

Luxury to Cape Town: the First Class Main Lounge and Gallery aboard the *Pretoria Castle*. (Union-Castle Line)

The 28,582-ton *Pendennis Castle*, commissioned in 1959, began a new generation of bigger, faster and finer Union-Castle mail ships. (ALF Collection)

From left to right: *Good Hope Castle*, *Reina Del Mar* and *Edinburgh Castle*, laid-up and idle during the maritime strike at Southampton in May–June 1966. (Southern Newspapers Ltd)

Pippa Gordon-Jones had a personal connection to Union Castle: her great-grandparents were in the British Colonial Service back in its regal heyday, in and around the First World War. They travelled with trunks, a nurse for their children and a maid. Her great-grandfather did well evidently – he had the imposing title of Deputy High Commissioner of Zulu Affairs. Amidst their papers, years later, Pippa said she'd found some Union Castle menu cards from ships such as the *Llanstephan Castle* and *Balmoral Castle*, as well as from the maiden voyage (in 1922) of the *Arundel Castle*.

Graham Spurrier spent his young days practically 'commuting' between England and South Africa. He and his parents always sailed with the Union-Castle Line.

Union Castle was the Cunard of the African runs. They and their ships were legendary. We sailed aboard the *Winchester Castle*, *Athlone Castle*, *Pretoria Castle* and *Kenya Castle*. They were great ships – very, very British, of course. It was all very different from today's cruise liners. There was far less entertainment – and far more quiet time. We played deck games in the morning, took time to write letters in the writing room and then took long naps in the afternoon. The ships, I seem to remember, were very quiet from 2 to 4 in the afternoon.

Then the ships were like tombs. You could only hear the moaning of the engines and the rattling of the ship itself. But the thing I remember most is the mug of beef tea you were given at 11 every morning.

Alan Parkhurst watched the great ships from his boyhood home in Cape Town, like I did along the Hoboken (New York) waterfront.

I would see all the liners and I became well known in the local steamship offices and travel agents. I was always requesting visitor passes to the ships. There was Union Castle, Holland Africa Line, Lloyd Triestino, Ellerman Lines, Shaw Savill and other passenger ships. I also recall the two Farrell Lines combo ships [carrying 82 passengers each], the *African Enterprise & African Endeavor*. They were sleek, very low ships with beautifully modern interiors. Then there were the passengers of ships of Holland's Royal Interocean Liners. They were all classic ships with names like *Ruys*, *Tegelberg*, *Tjitjalengka* and *Tjinegara*. And when the Suez was closed for a time, we had lots of others like all the big P&O liners, which were rerouted. Later, I actually travelled in some of the ships: the *Winchester Castle* to the UK, on the maiden

Above left: Modern style: the lobby on board Portugal's *Infante Dom Henrique*, commissioned in 1961. (Companhia Colonial)

Above right: East African service: arriving from London, British India's *Kenya* loads at Mombasa. (British India Line)

voyage coastal segments for the new *Pendennis Castle* [1959] and the *Northern Star* [1962], and once took a Portuguese liner, the *Principe Perfeito*, from Cape Town all the way to Beira. But the *Perfeito* got stuck on a sandbar at Beira and all the passengers had to be flown back to Cape Town. But the ship I most wished I had sailed aboard was the *Dominion Monarch* of Shaw Savill. She was so special, so gorgeous. But one of my very best voyages in those years was on the *Victoria* of Lloyd Triestino. It was Cape Town to Venice. We went in first class and had the most wonderful food and service. We arrived in Venice on a cold winter's morning. There was this great mist over the city. It was like a magnificent Canaletto painting.

On a summertime tour from Africa of Europe, Alan also visited Cannes. He stopped in the Italian Line office, which he said had the most beautiful model of the flagship *Andrea Doria* in the front window. 'But there was this great commotion in the office,' he added. 'It was July 26th 1956 and news had just arrived that the *Andrea Doria* sank.'

Britain's Ellerman Lines had four very fine combo ships that carried 100 passengers each and sailed between London and South and East Africa. Alan recalled:

They were truly all-first class. Just superb ships. They were fitted out like grand English country houses. The *City of York & City of Exeter* were the best. The other two, the *City of Port Elizabeth* and *City of Durban*, were different and not quite as grandly decorated. They were hugely popular ships and often had lots of lords and ladies among their passengers.

Opposite. Clockwise from top left:

The magnificent *Queen Elizabeth*, the world's largest liner, departing from New York in the 1950s. (ALF Collection)

Bon voyage: the *Queen Mary* departs from New York's Pier 90. (Anton Logvinenko)

28 ½ knots: crossing on the *Queen Mary*. (ALF Collection)

The mighty *Queen Elizabeth* departs from Southampton on another five-day crossing to New York. (Mick Lindsay Collection)

The 83,673grt *Queen Elizabeth* prepares to depart from
Southampton's Ocean Terminal. (ALF Collection)

Laid-up and for sale, Cunard sisters *Carmania* and *Franconia* at Southampton, 1972. (ALF Collection)

Noontime sailing: the *Constitution* departs for the Mediterranean. (ALF Collection)

American Export Lines' *Atlantic* is shifted from New York's Pier 84 to the adjoining Pier 86. (Mick Lindsay Collection)

The mighty *United States* makes another noontime departure from New York.
(Mick Lindsay Collection)

Sailing day for the *United States*.
(Mick Lindsay Collection)

The *Independence* seen off Cannes.
(Mick Lindsay Collection)

Italy's *Andrea Doria*. (Italian Line)

The *France* of the French Line.
(French Line)

Greek Line's *Arkadia*. (ALF Collection)

The *Independence* at New York.
(ALF Collection)

French Line's *Flandre*.
(ALF Collection)

Another view of the *France*.
(ALF Collection)

Sweden's handsome *Gripsholm*
with her masts tipped for bridge
clearance in the Kiel Canal.
(ALF Collection)

The *Bremen* departs from Southampton. (Mick Lindsay Collection)

The *Statendam* and the *Queen Elizabeth* (behind) are
berthed at Southampton. (Mick Lindsay Collection)

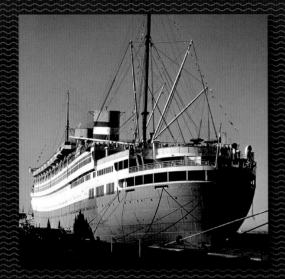

Clockwise from above left:

The classic lines and beauty of the *Nieuw Amsterdam*, seen here at Copenhagen during a summer cruise. (ALF Collection)

The 642ft-long *Statendam* berthed at Bermuda. (ALF Collection)

The renowned *Ile de France* at Pier 88, New York. (ALF Collection)

Rotterdam aerial: from left to right – *Westerdam*, *Nieuw Amsterdam* and *Rotterdam*. (ALF Collection)

A late morning departure for the *Liberte*. (ALF Collection)

The *Michelangelo* and her sister were capped by twin lattice, cage-like funnels. (Mick Lindsay Collection)

Clockwise from above left:

French artist Albert Brenet's brilliant depiction of the mighty *France* at New York. (Moran Towing & Transportation Co.)

During her world cruise in the winter of 1972, the *France* is seen at Circular Quay, Sydney. (French Line)

Afternoon sailing from Pier 84, New York, for Home Lines' *Homeric*. (ALF Collection)

Home Lines' *Italia*, the former *Kungsholm* of 1928, at Southampton. (ALF Collection)

Home Lines' *Italia* spent her winters cruising to the Caribbean. (Mick Lindsay Collection)

The stately *Vulcania* of the Italian Line. (Mick Lindsay Collection)

Clockwise from above left:

The *Leonardo da Vinci* departing on a March afternoon in 1973. (Author's Collection)

The mighty *Raffaello* anchored off Cannes. (ALF Collection)

Passing at sea: the New York-bound *Michelangelo* passes the Mediterranean-bound *Raffaello* in mid-Atlantic. (Italian Line)

Completed in 1936, Poland's *Batory* seen at
Pier 88, New York, in 1950. (Author's Collection)

Westbound crossing on the *Stefan Batory*
(ex-*Maasdam*). (ALF Collection)

Greek Line's *Arkadia* had been the three-funnel *Monarch of Bermuda* in her previous life. (Mick Lindsay Collection)

The 20,500-ton *Arkadia* is at anchor during a cruise, with Cunard's *Caronia* to the left. (ALF Collection)

The *France* arrives at the Ocean Terminal, Southampton.
(Mick Lindsay Collection)

Above: The Holland America combo ship *Dinteldyk* in the River Thames. (Mick Lindsay Collection)

Below: At Genoa (from top to bottom): *Raffaello*, the Bulgarian cruise ship *Varna* and the *Augustus*. (ALF Collection)

The splendid *Giulio Cesare* at New York. (ALF Collection)

The Costa Line flagship *Eugenio 'C'* was commissioned in 1966. (ALF Collection)

Blue Star Line's *Paraguay Star*, seen at the top of the Royal
Victoria Dock, London. (Mick Lindsay Collection)

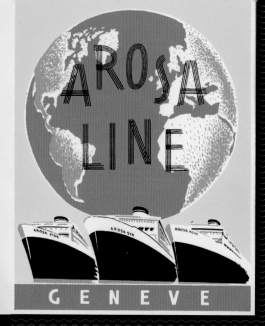

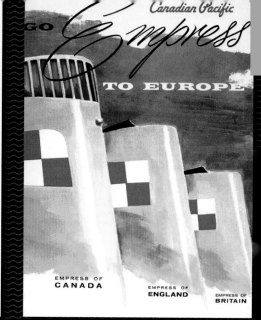

Clockwise from above left:

Arosa Line poster, 1955.
(Author's Collection)

A Cunard advertisement, 1955.
(Author's Collection)

Crossing on Canadian Pacific, 1962.
(Author's Collection)

Sailing to Europe on the French Line, 1952.
(Author's Collection)

Tourist class on Greek Line's *New York*, 1956.
(Author's Collection)

the Caribbean, 1951. (Author's Collection)

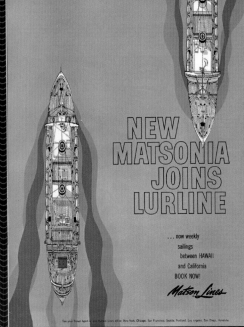

Matson Lines to Hawaii, 1957. (Author's Collection)

Far right: Off to the East: Anchor Line to India and Pakistan from Liverpool. (Author's Collection)

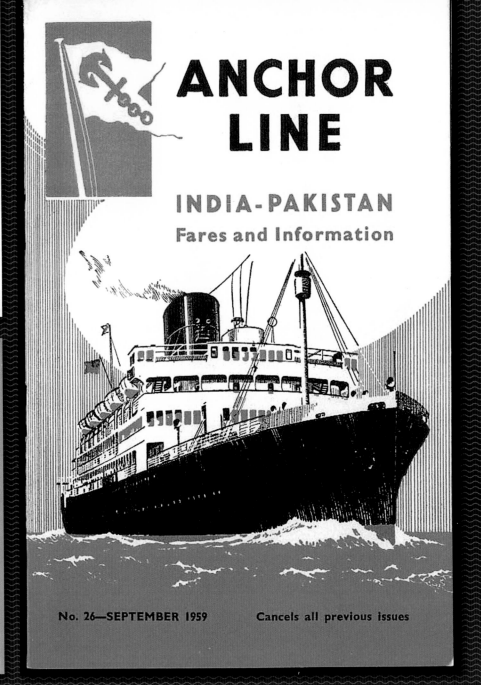

ANCHOR LINE

INDIA-PAKISTAN
Fares and Information

No. 26—SEPTEMBER 1959   Cancels all previous issues

A collection of baggage tags and company logos

P&O to Australia.
(Author's Collection)

A tourist class tag for the *France*. (Author's Collection)

French Line

"FRANCE"

LE HAVRE SOUTHAMPTON NEW YORK

Cᴵᴱ Gᴸᴱ TRANSATLANTIQUE

CLASSE TOURISTE
BAGAGE DE CABINE

P&O

NORWAY N·A·L DENMARK
Carefree Cruises
Norwegian America Line

NAME _____

SHIP _____

SAILING DATE _____ ROOM NUMBER _____

NEW YORK · BERGEN · BERGEN

PORT OF LANDING _____

MESSAGERIES MARITIMES

AGBL 580 - 8E - 12/66

M.M

CABINE

Norwegian America Line
to and from Norway.

France's 'Messageries

Anti-clockwise from above left:

British India Line's three-class *Karanja* sailed between South and East Africa and India. (ALF Collection)

The 14,000-ton *Aureol* was the flagship of the Elder Dempster Lines and used on the Liverpool–West Africa run. (Author's Collection)

The former *Pretoria Castle* was restyled in 1966 as the *SA Oranje*. (Mick Lindsay Collection)

The veteran *Carnarvon Castle* at Southampton. She dated from 1926. (Mick Lindsay Collection)

Anti-clockwise from top left:

Sleek, long and modern, the 760ft-long *Pendennis Castle* is seen at Cape Town. (Mick Lindsay Collection)

Flagship of the famed Union-Castle Line, the inbound *Windsor Castle* at Southampton. (Mick Lindsay Collection)

The former *Transvaal Castle* is seen here in 1966 as the restyled *SA Vaal*. (Mick Lindsay Collection)

The combo liner *City of Durban* of Ellerman Lines seen at Cape Town. (Dave Vincent Collection, courtesy of Mick Lindsay)

A rare view of Soviet liners at Odessa – the *Admiral Nakhimov* is berthed, the *Rossia* is just arriving. (Author's Collection)

The Soviet liner *Rossia* takes on passengers in a Black Sea port. (Mick Lindsay Collection)

Royal Interocean Lines' *Tegelberg* and a Maersk Line freighter berthed at Singapore. (John Bone Collection)

Used on the London–Far East run, the 1939-built *Canton* takes a break at the London Docks. (Mick Lindsay Collection)

P&O's popular *Arcadia* at Vancouver.
(Tim Noble Collection)

Another P&O liner, the *Iberia*, loading at the Pyrmont Docks, Sydney. (Tim Noble Collection)

Completed in 1950, the *Chusan* is at Circular Quay, Sydney. A rare image. (Tim Noble Collection)

The *Orion* in her final months, being used as a floating hotel at Hamburg. (Mick Lindsay Collection)

The mast-less *Orsova* at Aden. (Tim Noble Collection)

The 709ft-long *Oronsay* gets a 'touch up' at San Francisco. (ALF Collection)

The *Himalaya* docked at
Melbourne. (Tim Noble Collection)

The superb *Oriana* was the fastest
liner ever on the UK–Australia run.
(ALF Collection)

Ready for her sea trials, the mighty *Canberra* at the Harland & Wolff shipyard, Belfast, in the winter of 1961. (ALF Collection)

Seen here arriving at Sydney, the *Canberra* was the largest liner in regular service to Australia. (ALF Collection)

A busy day at Yokohama, 1966: the *Chitral*, *Sagaford* and *Canberra* berthed together. (Anton Logvinenko)

The stunning *Canberra* had an almost timeless sense of design.
(Mick Lindsay Collection)

Homeward from Australia: a view from the port bridge wing on board the *Himalaya*. (World Ship Society)

An idyllic afternoon: at sea in the South Pacific aboard the *Arcadia*. (Kay Stephens)

The *Orsova*, *Oriana* and the freighter *Newcastle Star* together at Melbourne. (John Bone Collection)

The *Oronsay*, seen here in her original corn-coloured hull, was completed in 1951. (Tim Noble Collection)

P&O-Orient Lines' *Oronsay* was completed in 1951. (Mick Lindsay Collection)

Looking forward from the stern of the *Oronsay* while berthed at Sydney. (World Ship Society)

Clockwise from right:

The *Oronsay* and *Australis* docked at Melbourne. (World Ship Society)

Shaw Savill Line's handsome *Dominion Monarch* berthed in the Royal Docks, London. (Mick Lindsay Collection)

A rare image of a chance meeting: the *Dominion Monarch* of 1939 meets the new *Southern Cross* of 1955. (Anton Logvinenko)

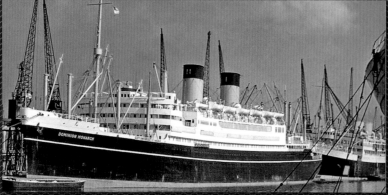

A busy day at Melbourne – the *Oronsay* (left), *Fairstar* (middle) and *Australis* (right). Another rare view. (World Ship Society)

A rare image of P&O's *Arcadia* and the *Guglielmo Marconi* of Lloyd Triestino at Melbourne. (World Ship Society)

A rare image of the Lloyd Triestino liners *Guglielmo Marconi* and the *Europa* berthed at Las Palmas. (Anton Logvinenko)

92

The *Australis* of Chandris Lines, berthed at Sydney. (Frank Andrews Collection)

The *Achille Lauro* and the *Michelangelo* undergoing repairs at a Genoa shipyard. (ALF Collection)

The *Patris* of Chandris Lines departs from Melbourne, with the *Achille Lauro* berthed behind. (Frank Andrews Collection)

New Zealand Shipping Co.'s *Rangitata* in the Royal Albert Dock, London in a view dated 8 March 1958. (Kenneth Wrightman Collection, courtesy of Mick Lindsay)

Orient Overseas Lines' *Oriental Jade* seen at San Francisco in this photo dated January 1966. (Author's Collection)

In 1963, New Zealand Shipping Co.'s *Rangitoto* calls at Melbourne on a special visit. (Tim Noble Collection)

The *President Cleveland* departs
for the Far East. (ALF Collection)

The beautiful *Lurline* at San
Francisco. (ALF Collection)

EXOTIC PORTS: THE MIDDLE AND FAR EAST

4

'We even had maharajas on the Anchor Line ships – the *Caledonia*, *Cilicia* and *Circassia* – on our trips to and from Bombay,' recalled the late John Philipps, a crew member with Liverpool-based Anchor. 'They would be visiting Britain, no doubt particularly to London. They travelled with entourages, lots of luggage, cases just for jewels and even sword-carrying bodyguards. Except for dinner, they sometimes rarely left their staterooms, the largest on board of course. But being all one-class, we also carried young Indians bound for schooling in Britain.'

Graham Hollick remembered:

It was the last of the old Empire, the fragments of the great colonial age. My parents lived in India and stayed on after independence in 1947. They remained in India until the early Sixties, but there were periodic trips home to the UK. I remember sailing on P&O, on the *Chusan*, *Stratheden* and *Orcades*, and on the Anchor Line, on the *Circassia*. They were classic British passenger liners – lots of lino floors, polished veneers, stuffed chairs and wicker, yes lots of wicker. But in contrast, even great contrast, was Lloyd Triestino and their two, very smart, almost sparkling ships *Asia* and *Victoria*. They called in at Bombay as part of their Italy-Far East sailings, and we could connect by train between Italy and the UK. They had much more modern decor and fittings, finer food and thorough air-conditioning. They were very smart looking ships: all-white, rather rakish and with domed funnels. My parents used to call them the 'Italian yachts'.

Blue Funnel had a quartet of thirty-passenger combo ships – the *Peleus*, *Pyrrhus*, *Patroclus* and *Perseus* – on the UK–Far East run until 1965. Nick Newman was a crew member and recalled, 'In the Fifties, we still carried the old Empire builders – the merchants, traders and businessmen. They used the long sea voyages as a rest. Life on board was comfortable, but very quiet, very tranquil.'

Age of Empire: P&O's *Corfu* and her sister *Carthage* on the long-distance run between London and the Far East. (P&O)

British shipboard decor: the First Class Main Lounge in first class aboard P&O's *Chusan*. She carried 1,026 passengers, divided between 475 in first class and 551 in tourist class. (Rich Turnwald Collection)

The smart-looking *Asia* departing from Cape Town. (Robert Pabst)

Royal Interocean Lines' *Boissevain* on her final visit to Cape Town in 1969. (Robert Pabst)

Holland's Royal Interocean Lines never actually went to the homeland, but traded in more distant waters. Their mainline service was one of the most extensive of all passenger ship services: Far East–Southeast Asia–Africa–South America. Six passenger ships were used: three larger sisters at 14,200 tons each, the *Boissevain*, *Ruys* and *Tegelberg*; the 11,000-ton *Tjitjalengka*; the 9,200-ton *Tjisadane*; and finally the 9,000-ton *Tjinegara*. The routing began at Yokohama and Kobe in Japan, and then continued to Hong Kong, Manila, Singapore, Port Swettenham, Penang, Mauritius, Lourenco Marques, Durban, East London, Port Elizabeth, Cape Town, Rio de Janeiro, Santos, Montevideo and Buenos Aires. Ships such as the 561ft-long *Boissevain* carried just over 100 passengers in first class and then 331 in other classes. As a sample voyage, the *Boissevain* departed from Yokohama on 13 November 1963 and reached Buenos Aires on 14 January. Fares for the full voyage ranged from $780 in a first-class suite to $450 in the least expensive first-class double, an inside room without a private bath. The latter equated to a daily fare of $8 per person.

Other lines that served Mid and Far East routes in 1960 included the likes of British India, Bibby Line, Henderson Line, Hamburg American-North German Lloyd, East Asiatic Co. and Lloyd Triestino. P&O stopped its regular service to Bombay and the Far East by 1970. By then, almost all other passenger lines in Far- and Mid-Eastern services were gone as well.

A long-retired couple remembered Liverpool from its days as a great seaport, one crammed with ships including some notable passenger ships. Among them were ships that sailed off to exotic, far-away ports in the Middle and Far East – to Karachi, Bombay, Rangoon, Penang and Hong Kong. There were the likes of the Anchor Line, Bibby Line, Blue Funnel Line and Henderson Line. Decades later, the couple shared their sentimentally reflective poem about shipping at Liverpool:

THE DOCKS

Gone are the docks
That made young men's dreams come true

Lost are the skills
That gave them their chance

Grown old now those
Lucky young men and the girls they once knew

Gone are the ships
That were full of romance

MIGRANTS AND MILLIONAIRES: AUSTRALIA AND NEW ZEALAND

5

Passenger ship services bound for Australia boomed, especially with outward migrants in the post-war years and particularly in the 1950s and '60s. Australia wanted to increase its population and so, under various schemes and usually with reduced (and often much reduced) fares, tens of thousands left British and European shores each year. Britain itself sent out a huge share, several hundred thousand in all, and P&O and the Orient line (later merged as P&O-Orient Lines), had the biggest share. There were fifteen passenger ships in all among their liners used in the 1960s: *Orontes*, *Orion*, *Strathnaver*, *Strathaird*, *Strathmore*, *Stratheden*, *Orcades*, *Himalaya*, *Chusan*, *Oronsay*, *Arcadia*, *Iberia*, and *Orsova*. The biggest, fastest and fanciest of all was the 41,900-ton, 2,100-passenger *Oriana* in 1960, followed by the even bigger 45,700-ton, 2,300-passenger *Canberra* a year later.

Michael Kenyon grew up in Sydney in the 1950s and was soon lured to its great harbour to watch the many passenger ships then calling there. In a recent interview, he recalled many of those liners from a great variety of shipping lines: P&O, Shaw Savill, Lloyd Triestino, Chandris, Lauro, Matson and even the smaller Australian passenger ships. He remembered:

I became seriously interested in 1961, the same time as the maiden arrival in Sydney of the innovative *Canberra*. She was an exciting ship – very different and certainly very big. The *Canberra* seemed to be always in port. She was so modern, so up-to-date, so suggestive of the future. To Australians, the *Canberra* was almost startling. The earlier P&O-Orient liners were conventional and very period – they were very chintzy and leather sofas and wicker in style. The *Canberra* and her look and decor were far more modern. She seemed to jump decades. And she was a big hit from the start. She had huge press coverage from the start. Liners were very newsworthy then and there were shipping reporters at all the

Right: A heroic return: the *Canberra* returns to Southampton in July 1982 following valiant service during the Falklands War. (P&O)

Below left: Rainy day: P&O's *Iberia* berthed at Vancouver. (ALF Collection)

Below right: The *Himalaya*, one of P&O's most popular post-war liners, departs from Cape Town. (Alex Duncan)

Above left: The First Class Lounge on P&O's *Himalaya*, 1949. (Richard Turnwald Collection)

Above right: Dubbed 'the Australia Room', this scene shows the reading and writing room on board the 1,159-passenger *Himalaya*. (Richard Turnwald Collection)

Left: The First Class Drawing Room on board P&O's 1954-built *Iberia*. (Richard Turnwald Collection)

Cheerful send-off: the veteran *Strathnaver* departs from Sydney. (P&O)

The handsome *Orion* berthed at Hobart, Tasmania. (P&O)

local newspapers. The *Oriana* was new and big and important as well. But she was more traditional, I felt, and largely an Orient Line ship in style and design whereas *Canberra* was more P&O. But I do well remember that the Monkey Bar in first class on the *Oriana* was my favourite public room on a liner back then.

P&O had several routings to and from Australia by the 1960s. There was the traditional run via Suez: London or Southampton to Gibraltar, sometimes Naples and Piraeus (to take on Italian and Greek migrants), Port Said, Aden, Colombo, Fremantle, Melbourne and Sydney. Homeward voyages sometimes included a stop at Marseilles. Then there were sailings via the South African Cape and others by way of Panama, including calls at the North American West Coast: Vancouver, San Francisco and Los Angeles – there was even the occasional routing to and from the Far East.

Michael Kenyon recalled:

> The earlier ships – *Orcades*, *Himalaya*, *Chusan* (built for the UK-Far East run, but which started to call in Australia in 1963), *Oronsay*, *Arcadia*, *Iberia* and *Orsova* – were all lovely ships with country house interiors in first class. With big chairs and sofas, they actually looked like your parents' home. The Orient Line ships were slightly different from P&O, perhaps a bit more modern. But altogether they were all quite similar. They all had that classic Fifties British passenger ship decor. I do also remember the pre-war *Strathmore* and *Stratheden*. They had huge urns in the first class writing room and elsewhere lots of wicker furniture. But comparatively, there was a huge contrast by the Sixties between the P&O-Orient ships and the decoratively more modern Italians and Americans.

Shaw Savill Line was a British alternative to P&O and, by 1960, had a rather eclectic fleet: the pre-war *Dominion Monarch*; the innovative, engines-aft *Southern Cross* of 1955; and four eighty-five-passenger combination passenger-cargo ships: *Athenic*, *Ceramic*, *Corinthic* and *Gothic*.

> The *Southern Cross* was certainly innovative with her aft funnel, midships pool and all-one class configuration. But she was not especially popular ship among her crew. Said to be 'hard to work,' she was dubbed the 'Suffering Cross'. Inside, she was adequately pleasant and comfortable, but also rather basic in places. I do recall lots of exposed pipes along corridors and in cabins. The *Northern Star* [added in 1962] was a larger version, but also had nothing very striking about her decor. She did, however, have mechanical problems for all of her life. She was even late on her maiden voyage.

Martin Shawcross sailed with the Shaw Savill Line for several years in the 1960s and added:

> It was a wonderful time – a young man, the sea, far-away places. I served first on the *Southern Cross*. She was a unique ship for her time – all passengers and no cargo. And she was all-one class – no upper-deck first class. We did continuous 2 ½-month trips around-the-world. We had lots of migrants going out to Australia and then Australian tourists & backpackers on the trips returning to the UK. But it was all go – and unlike today's world cruises. We rarely remained overnight in the ports of call. We were, in ways, like a train. I also served aboard the *Athenic* and *Corinthic*, big passenger-cargo ships that carried only about 85 passengers each. They were used on a long, rather slow service out of London to ports in New Zealand and sometimes over to Australia. Cargo determined everything. We loaded lots of meat and wool, and brought these home to the UK. Outwards, we took British manufactured goods. The passengers tended to be older – retirees, tourists, the occasional businessman

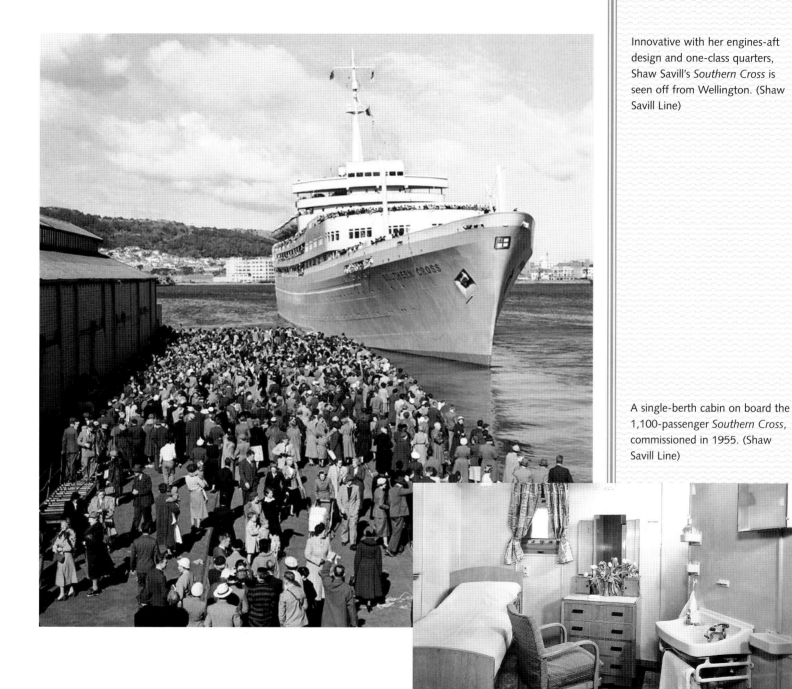

Innovative with her engines-aft design and one-class quarters, Shaw Savill's *Southern Cross* is seen off from Wellington. (Shaw Savill Line)

A single-berth cabin on board the 1,100-passenger *Southern Cross*, commissioned in 1955. (Shaw Savill Line)

Above left: Passengers and cargo: Shaw Savill's *Athenic* carried up to eighty-five one-class passengers on the UK–New Zealand run. (Shaw Savill Line)

Above right: A royal voyage: the *Athenic's* sister *Gothic* was selected in 1953–54 to take HM Queen Elizabeth II on a post-Coronation world voyage. Painted in white and dressed in flags, the 561ft *Gothic* is seen here at Wellington. (ALF Collection)

Right: Specially refitted and painted in all-white, the *Gothic* sails off the English south coast, bound for Jamaica, where Queen Elizabeth II will join for a long, post-Coronation trip around the world. (Shaw Savill Line)

Opposite: After strenuous war duties, the *Dominion Monarch* sails from the Queens Wharf at Wellington on 5 March 1949. (ALF Collection)

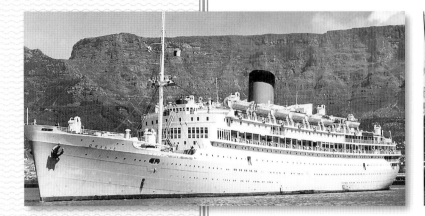

Above left: One of Holland's most beloved liners, the *Oranje*, is seen at Cape Town. (Alex Duncan)

Above right: The smart-looking *Willem Ruys* berthed at Rotterdam between voyages out to the Dutch East Indies. (Cronican-Arroyo Collection)

or government official. Life aboard was comparatively very quiet – long days at sea, quiet afternoons and very simple evening entertainment. I remember frog racing as one event.

Two well-known Dutch shipping lines, Royal Rotterdam Lloyd and the Nederland Line, ran three liners in coordinated, monthly around-the-world services that called at Sydney, Melbourne and Wellington beginning in the late 1950s. They were the *Johan van Oldenbarnevelt*, *Oranje* and *Willem Ruys*. Michael Kenyon remembered:

I saw the *John van Oldenbarnevelt* during her last season to Australia [1962] and, with lots of coffee-colored mahogany and carvings, her decor was very heavy and very, very dark. In contrast, the *Oranje* and *Willem Ruys* were much lighter in decor and also much brighter. They even used more modern, 1950s lighting. An added notation: In 1959, the *Oranje* became the first foreign-flag ship to make a cruise from Sydney. She was, of course, well known, having been a Royal Australian Naval hospital ship during World War II.

Under the French flag, Messageries Maritimes, a long-established shipping line later integrated into the current CMA CGM, a giant container ship operator, ran a passenger service south in the Pacific to Sydney. The routing was from Marseilles to the Caribbean and Panama and then to the South Pacific. Two passenger-cargo liners, the *Caledonien* and *Tahitien*, carrying some 241 passengers in three classes, were used and then joined by a third ship, the *Oceanien*. Michael Kenyon remembered them:

I recall visiting the *Caledonien* on a rainy morning at Sydney in the 1960s. The ship had just arrived and had a peculiar smell. But what was it? Otherwise, the ship had a very

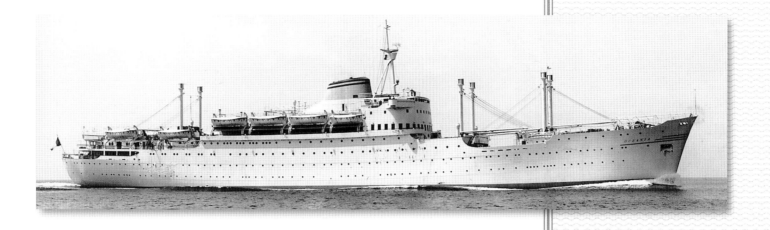

The three-class *Oceania*, used on the Italy–Australia run for Lloyd Triestino. (Robert Pabst)

nice first class, but new second class accommodation by then and an improved third class. The *Oceanien*, the former *Noordam*, had not changed. She was still a Holland America, still a Dutch ship. And there was the little *Polynesie* [3,700 tons], which carried only 36 passengers and which was in Sydney every three weeks. She ran something of a supply service to Noumea and the New Hebrides. On board, the *Polynesie* was very tiny – with simple, small cabins, a cramped lounge and steep stairwells and narrow corridors.

Italian ship owners had an especially strong interest in Australia, primarily because of the highly profitable outward migrant trade. Lloyd Triestino was perhaps the most prominent of these firms. Michael recalls:

I remember their earlier liners, the *Australia*, *Neptunia* and *Oceania*, for having lots of highly polished lino floors. And that Lloyd Triestino departures were always very loud. There were lots of Italians yelling and screaming and even crying. It was a very chaotic atmosphere. The *Guglielmo Marconi* and *Galileo Galilei* arrived in 1963 and were big improvements. Not only beautiful-looking ships, they were much smarter in decor and style. Their first-class quarters were especially lovely and, being Italian, they had attractive aft lido decks with umbrella-lined swimming pools.

Genoa-based Sitmar Line was also actively involved in low-fare Australian service.

An interesting company, they were known initially for having smaller, converted passenger ships with high capacities. The *Fairsea* and *Fairsky* had been small aircraft carriers during the War while the *Castel Felice* dated from 1930. The *Fairsea* was especially interesting

The *Guglielmo Marconi* (seen here) and her sister *Galileo Galilei* were great favourites on the Italy–Australia run. The 27,900-ton sisters were completed in 1963. (ALF Collection)

to me. She was long, low, had a wide, flat funnel and, at only 11,000 tons, could carry over 1,400 passengers. When the new *Fairstar* arrived in 1964, she was a big step up. She wasn't luxurious, but very comfortable, well decorated and had such amenities as a two-deck high lounge and twin outdoor pools. At sailings, Sitmar were always very crowded. The Company was also very, very practical – their ships arrived in Sydney early in the morning and then sailed late that same night. Little time was wasted.

Based at Naples, Flotta Lauro, or the Lauro Line to many, began with two passenger ships, the 14,700-ton *Roma* and *Sydney*, which had been small aircraft carriers during the Second World War. Lauro took a great leap forward, however, when they introduced two luxury liners, the lavishly converted *Angelina Lauro* (the former Dutch *Oranje*) and *Achille Lauro* (ex-*Willem Ruys*). Michael Kenyon also remembers these ships:

The *Roma* and *Sydney* were very comfy ships and, typically Italian, had lots of lino floors. I never managed to get on board *Angelina Lauro*, but what a ship! I always thought *Oranje* was a good-looking ship, but what an incredible transformation those architects made with a new

Outbound from Yokohama for
ports in South America, the *Brazil
Maru* has a high-spirited departure.
(Hisashi Noma Collection)

bow, streamlined superstructure and that wonderful funnel with its nod to the *Michelangelo* funnels! I did, however, go on *Achille Lauro* early in her career. *Willem Ruys* was lovely inside, but as a Lauro liner, the décor was totally different – and was very Italian and very stylish.

Yet another Italian liner company, the Cogedar Line, built their fortunes in the migrant and low-fare tourist trades. Michael Kenyon added:

Cogedar was, to me, a fascinating little company. They had the *Flaminia*, which had been a freighter built in 1922, but rebuilt to carry 1,024 passengers, all in one-class. She was a very basic ship, carrying migrants out to Australia and sometimes chartered to transport Australian troops. Evidently, the ship was less than pleasing. On one voyage, many jumped ship at Suez. The *Aurelia* was actually a quirky ship in ways, but an improvement in Cogedar's migrant and around-the-world service. She was even made a short cruise from Sydney in 1960. But the *Flavia*, the greatly rebuilt former *Media* of Cunard [a combination passenger-cargo ship with 250 berths], was a huge step for Cogedar. She was modern, nicely decorated and aptly joined the 'new Italians' on the Australian run in the early Sixties.

Michael adds:

> The *Flavia* is one of my all-time favourite ships and I think rather underrated. The conversion from *Media* was done to a very high standard, for example the majority of cabins had private facilities unlike the other ships at the time like *Canberra* and *Oriana*, *Fairstar*, *Ellinis*, *Northern Star* etc.
>
> By the time *Flavia* entered service, Cogedar had sent the *Aurelia* on 2 cruises from Australia (in August 1960 and January 1962) and I suspect Cogedar saw a future for the *Flavia* in cruising. In April 1963 on her third voyage, she made a thirty-six-day cruise to Japan and Hong Kong, and then on her next voyage made another shorter cruise to north Queensland. In all, over the period 1963-1968, she made fourteen cruises from Australia varying in duration from two weeks to forty-five days (the latter to Hawaii and Tahiti).
>
> Internally she was very smart with the highlight being the twin-level Riviera lounge (pre-dating a similar room on *Fairstar*), good open deck space with two pools and functional cabins. It's no wonder that she was snapped up by Costa in 1968 for the Bahamas cruise service.

Australia needed workers, and few liner companies benefited more than the Greek-owned Chandris Lines. Eventually they received the prized contract from the Australian government to carry migrants out to the likes of Fremantle, Melbourne and Sydney. It has been said that almost all of the large Greek population in Melbourne has some connection with Chandris and its passenger ships: *Patris*, *Ellinis*, *Australis* and *Britanis*. Even the veteran *Queen Frederica* was used at times. Michael Kenyon recalled:

> Having been the *Lurline*, the converted *Ellinis* was little changed except for her exterior and that her capacity was more than doubled from 760 to 1,600. And it was the same for the *Australis*. She was the former *America* and was still basically a United States Lines' Atlantic liner. But her capacity was more than doubled as well by Chandris – from 1,000 to over 2,200.

There was also the London-based New Zealand Shipping Co., which operated big combination passenger-cargo liners to Auckland and Wellington, and Holland's Royal Interocean Lines.

> The *Tjiuwangi* and *Tjiluwah* of Royal Interocean were lovely ships – and actually quite beautiful in first class. There was an impressive sort of grand stairwell and a garden lounge with greenery and wicker chairs. Ironically, even if their next lives, the two ships remained linked to Australia. As the *Kota Bali*, the former *Tjiwangi*, cruised out of Fremantle while the *Kota Singapura*, ex-*Tjiluwah*, ran a so-called 'ship-jet' service between Fremantle and Singapore. A third Royal Interocean passenger ship, the *Straat Banka*, also called regularly at Sydney. Carrying only 40 passengers in all-first-class quarters, she had a rather unusual routing

– from India to Southeast Asia and Australia [between Bombay, Cochin, Colombo, Penang, Singapore, Djakarta, Brisbane, Sydney and Melbourne]. A smart-looking ship that was typically Dutch and always immaculate, she was never-the-less [*sic.*] fumigated by Australian authorities upon arrival. There was always a fear she had been infested while in India.

Another long popular service was between Australia and the Far East. Companies on this route included Eastern and Australian, China Navigation Co. Ltd and Dominion Far East Line.

Australia itself had a mini fleet of coastal liners in 1960, with ships such as the *Manoora*, *Bulolo*, *Malaita*, *Wanganella*, *Kanimbla* and the little passenger ships belonging to the Western Australia Government. Michael Kenyon also remembered these smaller Australian passenger ships:

The *Kanimbla* ran between Melbourne, Sydney, Brisbane, Townsville and Cairns, and also used to run an annual 42-day cruise from Australia to ports in the Far East as well as an annual boy scout jamboree cruise. She was a nice little ship, but when she returned after being sold as the *Oriental Queen*, she was passed [*sic.*] her best and even rundown. Other ships such as the *Bulolo* and *Wanganella* were interesting, even quite lovely in ways, but hardly remarkable. On board, and while comfortable, they tended to look the same.

Some people have enjoyed very diverse travels – in particular, sea travels. Now in his 80s, Marco Roccalia was born in Switzerland and, as a teenager and young man, joined his professor father in making long journeys by sea on some very varied ships. His father knew lots about passenger ships back in the 1950s and '60s and closely followed their itineraries and schedules. Together, they'd make long summer trips, sometimes completely around the world. Marco's father would map the connecting ships in the various ports. He recalled:

When we lived in northern Italy, we would sail from Genoa. We took the North German Lloyd combo ship *Frankfurt* from there out to Hong Kong. The ship was small but very beautiful, could carry over 80 passengers, but there were as few as 25 on our trip. With lots of stops, it took five weeks from Genoa to Hong Kong. From Hong Kong, we crossed to Japan, Hawaii and finally San Francisco on the *President Wilson*. An American ship, I recall it being immaculate – shining everywhere! Afterward, we crossed America by train and eventually took the *Leonardo da Vinci* home from New York to Genoa. The entire trip took almost four months.

Another trip from Genoa took us back to the Far East, an area which interested my father. The East was still quite different, quite exotic even and not as modern nor as busy as today. We left Genoa on the *Guglielmo Marconi* and sailed through the Suez Canal to Sydney. After a week or so in Sydney, we caught the *Mariposa* and sailed up to San Francisco. From there, we took P&O's *Chusan* across to Yokohama, Kobe and Hong Kong. At Hong Kong, we later switched to the *Cathay*, another combination-style passenger-cargo ship carrying only about 200 passengers, which took us back to Australia, to Sydney. From Sydney, we returned home to Italy on the *Achille Lauro*.

Marco, his father and family later moved to New York City. From there, he and his father made three other long sea trips:

We took the *Argentina* from New York to Rio de Janeiro and from there we boarded a Dutch ship, the *Tegelberg*, and sailed to South Africa, Southeast Asia and finally to Hong Kong. Afterward, we crossed from Hong Kong to San Francisco on the *President Cleveland*. That trip, as I remember, took 4 ½ months.

The two other trips focused on Africa and then South America:

We crossed from New York to Southampton on the *Queen Elizabeth* and from there caught the *Pretoria Castle* to Cape Town and Durban in South Africa. Then we switched to another Union-Castle passenger ship, the *Rhodesia Castle*, and sailed along the East African coast, passed through Suez and the Mediterranean before finishing in London. We finally came home from Southampton to New York on the *Caronia*.

   The South American trip took about 2 ½ months. We sailed from New York to the Panama Canal and then south to Valparaiso on the *Santa Isabel*, a Grace Line ship that could carry about 50 or so passengers, but had only 14 on board our trip. From Chile, we later crossed over to Argentina and finally landed at Buenos Aires. We were supposed to sail north to the USA, from Buenos Aires to New Orleans, on the *Del Mar*, another ship with about 100 passenger berths. But there were some last-minute changes and instead we sailed to New York instead and on the far larger *Brasil*.

Marco has kept scrapbooks of his trips and to date has logged fifty or so cruises on the likes of Holland America, Cunard, Silversea, Regent and Crystal. He finishes: 'I keep up my father's tradition and travel by ship. I still love ships and the sea!'

   Many of these ships have left a strong and lasting impression on Australians, and they often played a part in family histories. George and Alice Shaw added: 'We live in Brisbane in a complex of flats. Each building has a name – the name of a liner: *Arcadia*, *Oriana* & *Oronsay*. We live in *Oronsay*. There's a fourth building, but it is named *Somerset* [but for a British freighter].'

CROSSING THE PACIFIC

6

Crossing the Pacific was looked after by several companies: the US-flag Matson and American President Lines, Japan's Mitsui-OSK Lines and, biggest and most diverse of all, the roving liners of P&O-Orient Lines.

The San Francisco-based Matson Line was very popular, especially for its California–Hawaii/South Pacific services, and continued in the passenger business until 1970. At its peak, by 1960, the Company had four passenger liners: *Lurline*, *Matsonia*, *Mariposa* and *Monterey*. 'My father was a captain with the Matson Line – on the *Lurline*, *Mariposa* & *Monterey*. They were such well known ships – a part of San Francisco, fixtures in the Pacific,' recalled Joann Bauer. 'It was a wonderful life. But when he was asked if he was ever close to sinking, he always said "I'd rather sink and go down with the ship than face those long Coast Guard hearings afterward".'

Holland's *Johan van Oldenbarnevelt*, berthed at Wellington, New Zealand. (Nedlloyd)

Above left: A rare image of the *Mariposa* arriving at San Francisco for the first time. (ALF Collection)

Above right: The *President Cleveland*, berthed at Hong Kong, with P&O-Orient's *Orsova* on the left. (ALF Collection)

Hawaiian tourism boomed after the Second World War and eventually required two liners, the 1931-built *Lurline* and her restored sister *Matsonia*. Matson also reopened its pre-war South Pacific–Australia service, running a regular service to Australia as part of forty-two-day itineraries. Handsome-looking ships converted from big, fast freighters, the 14,900-ton *Mariposa* and *Monterey* were very luxurious. They carried only 365 passengers each and all of them in first class quarters. 'The *Mariposa* and *Monterey* were considered very prestigious ships along the Sydney waterfront,' noted Michael Kenyon:

> They were shatteringly modern to Australians – and especially with their decorative style of American modern coupled with Polynesian themes. Their cabins were large, very comfortable and all of them with private bathrooms. And they had the best air-conditioning. I recall the 'high cool' of the *Mariposa* during an otherwise sweltering summer's day in Sydney. They also had a certain status and the dockers wore white doctor's jackets when handling them. The dockers were also given free lunches on board and so the two ships were especially well liked. Myself, I had my very first piece of American-style cheese cake while having lunch on the *Mariposa*.

Also based at San Francisco, American President Lines was interested in the Far East – to Yokohama, Kobe, Hong Kong and Manila – and had several liners: the *President Cleveland*, *President Wilson*, *President Hoover* and *President Roosevelt*. Cook and Mary Quinn recalled:

Our first cruise was not in the Caribbean or across the Atlantic, but across the Pacific. It was 1962 and we sailed from San Francisco to Hong Kong on the *President Hoover*. We had a few weeks there and then returned to the States on the *President Wilson*. It was American President Lines and all-American food and service. I still have a few menus. But life on a ship then was much more relaxed, even quiet. There were no lecturers or after-dinner production shows. I think we relied on our own entertainment more in those days. And there always seemed to be time for an afternoon nap – the whole ship seemed to rest and life on board become very, very quiet.

P&O-Orient Lines, as it was known in the early 1960s, had expanded its liner services to the West Coast of North America and offered numerous voyages, especially to and from Australia and the Far East. Hugh Markham lived in San Francisco and, being young and limited financially, enjoyed the low fares of P&O tourist-class accommodation:

American President Lines' San Francisco terminal in the late 1950s. The *President Cleveland* and three freighters are berthed in the foreground, the *President Wilson* behind. (Author's Collection)

Being a teacher, I had long summer vacations and P&O voyages seemed ideal. They had the most wonderful foldout schedules to faraway ports and, being affordable, I began to plan each summer – always using San Francisco as my base. Happy to say that I travelled on most of the P&O liners of that era. My first trip, in 1959, was to Australia – down on the *Orcades* and then home on the *Arcadia*. Later, I went to the Far East on the *Chusan* and then, during another summer, to Europe via Panama – out on the new *Canberra* and home on the *Orsova*. I also did a round-the-Pacific voyage on the *Himalaya* and a three-ship trip: the *Oronsay* to Australia, then the *Oriana* from Australia to the Far East and then home to San Francisco on the *Iberia*. P&O offered a wonderful shipboard experience for me: Lots of curries at meals, deck games, lots of young fellow passengers and charming, hardworking Indian stewards and waiters. And, of course, it was very, very British – the noon whistle, quizzes and afternoon tea. And which was my favourite ship? Well, I must say it was the *Arcadia*. She had this special charm and warmth that few other liners had or ever had.

P&O-Orient advertised their ships as the 'biggest bloom ships in the Pacific'. A couple from Fiji, but now living in Vancouver, first travelled on P&O-Orient in 1966. She emigrated from Suva on the *Oronsay*; he followed a few years later aboard the *Oriana*. 'Fifty years ago, they seemed like such big ships – and it seems so quaint these days, but they were divided between first class and tourist class.'

AFTERWORD

Almost all of the companies and the ships listed in this book are gone. They have been replaced by a multi-billion cruise industry, one in which some 25 million take to the seas every year. With over 200 cruise ships in service at the time of writing, over eighty new ships were either on order or under construction, including bigger and flashier ships.

As I completed this book, in the spring of 2017, Miami-based Royal Caribbean International's *Symphony of the Seas*, the largest liner ever, was ceremoniously floated out at her builders yard, STX at St Nazaire, France. Costing some $1.5 billion, the ship will break all records and weigh in at 230,000 gross tons, as well as measuring 1,188ft in length and 215ft in width. Due in service for the Miami–Caribbean line on seven-night cruises, she will have the largest capacity yet – 6,870 guests in all.

On eighteen decks, there are 2,775 staterooms, twenty-four passenger elevators and no less than seven on-board 'neighbourhoods' – named and themed as Central Park, Boardwalk, Royal Promenade, Pool and Sports Zone, Vitality at Sea, Entertainment Place and Youth Zone. Highlights are the Ultimate Abyss, a ten-storey slide; the Perfect Storm with a trio of water slides; and Splashaway Bay, a children's water park. There will be six dining areas and ten speciality restaurants.

Yes, the likes of the *Symphony of the Seas* will be extraordinary. She's special, innovative and sets a standard – a great and grand successor to these earlier Blue Water Liners.

BIBLIOGRAPHY

Dunn, Laurence, *Passenger Liners* (London: Adlard Coles Ltd, 2nd Ed., 1965).

Heine, Frank & Lose, Frank, *Great Passenger Ships of the World* (Hamburg, Germany: Koehlers Verlagsgesellschaft, 2010).

Miller, William H., *Floating Palaces: The Great Atlantic Liners* (Stroud, Gloucestershire: Amberley Publishing Co., 2010).

Miller, William H., *The Last Atlantic Liners: Getting There is Half the Fun* (Stroud, Gloucestershire: Amberley Publishing Co., 2011).

Miller, William H., *Transatlantic Liners 1945–80* (Newton Abbot, Devon: David & Charles Ltd, 1981).

Miller, William H., *Under the Red Ensign: British Passenger Liners of the '50s & '60s* (Stroud, Gloucestershire: The History Press, 2009).

Ocean & Cruise News (1980–2014), Northport, New York: World Ocean & Cruise Liner Society.

Official Steamship Guide (1951–63), New York City: Transportation Guides Inc.